AMERICAN FURNITURE

AMERICAN FURNITURE

JOHN S BOWMAN

Exeter Books

NEW YORK

A Bison Book

First published in USA 1985
by Exeter Books
Distributed by Bookthrift
Exeter is a trademark of Simon & Schuster, Inc.
New York, New York

ISBN 0-671-07578-0

Printed in Hong Kong

Page 1: *The Shaker Rocking Chair had a seat woven with tapes or splints.*

Pages 2-3: *The Barcelona Chair by Mies van der Rohe seems as contemporary today as it did when designed in 1929.*

This page: *A Stickley Dining Table and chairs show an interest in construction which was a hallmark of the Arts and Crafts Movement.*

TABLE OF CONTENTS

1
The Colonists' Furniture

A history of American furniture is of necessity a microcosm of the history of America. It is now accepted that the furniture made during each period reflects the resources – wood, metals, tools, etc – of the time; it reflects the people's economic, social, and political conditions (even international affairs: American furniture design has always tended to 'tread water' during wartime); and furniture also reflects those less tangible values and ideals – aesthetic, aspirational, even religious – that give the true texture to each period. Again, this is now universally accepted.

But there is another history that an account of American furniture now reflects, and that is history as it is studied and understood and written about by experts and professionals. That history has changed greatly during the last couple of decades, so that an up-to-date account of American furniture is now considerably different from one written, say, in 1955. Histories of American furniture written up to then often ended with the furniture made up to about 1830 – or up to 1900 at the latest. Such histories also tended to concentrate largely, if not solely, on 'High' styles – Queen Anne, Chippendale, Empire – which not so coincidentally were directly related to European styles and which were made, sold, and used in relatively limited parts of America – Boston, New York, Philadelphia, for instance, or New England and around Chesapeake Bay.

Of course such histories of American furniture were also reflecting the broader history of America as it was then regarded, and part of the problem was due to the sheer lack of information about other facets. But part of the problem was also due to a longstanding bias, unconscious or otherwise, that pervaded American history – a bias toward the elite and powerful, those who could be placed neatly into familiar (ie European) pigeonholes and those who had themselves recorded as well as 'made' history. Beyond that, there was a specific bias toward New England that long dominated histories of America and American furniture in particular.

So it was that until quite recently the seventeenth century in accounts of American history was often called 'the Pilgrim century' or 'the Puritan age,' as though seventeenth-century

America began with Plymouth and ended at the Massachusetts Bay Colony. In fact, the English themselves had an earlier successful colony in Virginia, while both the Spanish and the French had long preceded the English in North America – and even the Dutch had begun to settle the New Netherlands. By 1630, New Amsterdam was a town of 300 inhabitants and neat gabled houses that most certainly had many items of furniture, both imported and locally made. And the same was true for Jamestown, Virginia, which numbered some 866 colonists in 1620; admittedly, most of them were men who had little time for furniture, but the colony's sponsors had just begun to ship 'young and uncorrupt maids' to Jamestown, where they could be purchased as wives for 150 pounds of the best tobacco – and where wives came, furniture was sure to follow.

But as long as this is understood, there are indeed solid grounds for commencing a survey of American furniture with that made in the early New England settlements. For various reasons other colonies – Virginia, the Spanish, the French, the Dutch – did not produce either the quantities or the quality of furniture that would be saved by their later generations. Whereas the English colonists of Plymouth and Boston seem to have begun self-consciously saving their furniture from the first day ashore. Even if it is accepted that not all the pieces now claimed as having 'come over on the *Mayflower'* could have fit aboard, there are several pieces that do seem authentic. One is the wicker cradle, evidently made in Leyden, Holland, where the Pilgrims had lived some years before setting forth for the New World, a cradle believed to have been used by Peregrine White, the first baby born at Plymouth. And there is at least one chair, the one said to have belonged to Governor John Carver, that is now considered – because analysis shows its wood to be a European ash – to have been brought over from England.

But considering the size of the *Mayflower,* and all the early ships that brought colonists, it is hard to believe that much furniture was brought over. Rather, the colonists, – especially the first Pilgrims to arrive in Plymouth – greatly underestimated the severity of the climate in

---

Previous page: *Early American buildings and furniture such as those seen at Plimoth Plantation, both used the mortise-and-tenon frame in construction.*

A 'Carver' chair so-called for its resemblance to one owned by Governor John Carver, has no turned spindles beneath the arms or the rush seat.

the New World and they came with little else except personal possessions. Half of the first Plymouth colonists died that winter – 'wanting houses and other comforts' – while ten years later the first settlers of the Massachusetts Bay Colony had to 'burrow themselves in the Earth for their first shelter under some Hill-side.' And even when they wrote back to England to advise the next groups of colonists, these hardy New Englanders did not mention furniture. John Winthrop, the first governor of Massachusetts Bay Colony, wrote his wife in 1630 to tell her to bring such items as pewter, soap, axes, drinking horns, and leather bottles, while the Reverend Francis Higginson, the first minister at Salem, wrote that same year: 'Before you come . . . be sure to furnish yourselves with things fittest to be had . . . as meale for bread, malt for drinke, woolen and linnen cloath and leather for shoes, and all manner of carpenters tools, and a great deal of iron and steele to make nails, and locks for houses, and furniture [i.e. gear] for ploughs and carts, and glasse for windows, and many other things which were better for you to think of there than to want them here.' Arms and armor, in fact, had far higher priority for the early New Englanders than did furniture.

But carpenters' tools, as noted, were recognized as necessities, and from the very outset the colonists were aware of the apparently endless supplies of wood in the New World. In England and Europe, large tracts of woodland were 'locked up' in the estates of the gentry, but in the New World there was more wood than anyone could have imagined. At once the first New Englanders began to use it for houses, sheds, churches, and every kind of structure; they began to burn it for heating and cooking; they used it for making utensils, tools and containers (such as buckets and barrels); they used it for making carts and wagons and boats and ships. Naturally they also used it for their furniture. And even though the forests of New England were filled with pine, walnut, and maple, these early settlers preferred to make much of their furniture out of the oak that had been used for so long in England.

This same conservatism, this strong attachment to their English ways of doing things, would play a major part in the furniture that was made in New England – and well beyond the seventeenth century. The very tools that these first New England furniture makers used

Known as 'Wey Wood Turner's armchair' this chair has an unusual triangular seat and turned arms and finials.

were, after all, not much different from those used for centuries – even millennia: basic hammers, saws, chisels, planes, augers, compasses, and measures. These were the tools used more or less by all men who worked with wood. At most the furniture-makers might have planes with special edges or more delicate chisels, but there could not be much specialization in the early years in the New World. Coopers made barrels, and carpenters tended to make houses, and turners used lathes to make such pieces as spindles, balustrades, and bosses, and there were shipwrights, but all must have had to pitch in at times and do each other's work. (One of the best known of such jacks-of-all-trades was none other than John Alden, the cooper who married Priscilla Mullins.)

The furniture-makers in those early decades of the seventeenth century were known as 'joiners', for the primary method of constructing furniture, at least among the English of this time, was that of mortise-and-tenon joinery. The mortise is the hole chiseled and cut into one piece of wood, while the tenon is the tongue or protruding element shaped from another piece of wood so that it fits into the mortise; another small hole is then drilled (with the auger) through the mortised end and the tenon so that a whittled peg can secure the joint – thus the 'joiner.' Panels were fitted into slots on the basic frames. This kind of construction was used for making everything from houses to chests.

Relatively little hardware was used during these decades of the seventeenth century. Some

nails – forged by hand – were used, but no screws or glue. Hinges were often made of leather, but metal hinges were also used. The cruder varieties were made by blacksmiths in the colonies, but the finer metal elements were imported. Locks and escutcheon plates – the latter to protect the wood from the metal key – would often be imported in the early decades.

Above all, what the early English colonists imported was their knowledge of, familiarity with, dedication to the traditional types and

The flat tulip and sunflower carvings on this chest with two drawers are typical of the area near Wethersfield, Connecticut.

An oak and pine press cupboard from Massachusetts.

designs of furniture they knew in England. As it happens, the leaders of the Massachusetts Bay Colony – men such as John Winthrop, Thomas Dudley, Sir Richard Saltonstall, William Pynchon, and others – were men of some substance and undoubtedly had lived with furniture of some substance. But many of their followers, and most of the early Plymouth colonists, were not from the more prosperous levels of English society; they came from small towns, the remote counties, from the countryside. Their homes had oiled-paper for windows, not glass; they were used to open hearths, not chimneys; they often knew earthen floors, not wooden ones; they may have used some pewter for tableware but they probably used a lot of wooden utensils (and the fork was not even introduced into England until the first half of the seventeenth century); they probably sat on benches and stools as often as chairs; and many probably did not sleep on much more than mattresses or bunks. It was, in fact, still a medieval style of life, and much of the furniture that they did own and use in their English homes could be traced directly to medieval models.

If this relatively simple, even crude, type of furniture was the most common for many of the early English colonists, the furniture that was most prized and that thus survived tended to be the more fashionable and better-made. The furniture that these English regarded as the best was that they knew from the recent decades in England – namely, the Elizabethan and Jacobean styles. The former obviously takes its name from Queen Elizabeth, who reigned from 1558 to 1603 and set her stamp on everything produced during her age. The latter is derived from *Jacobus*, the Latin version of James, and as such refers to James I, King of England from 1603-1625; just like Elizabeth, he gave his name both to a particular period of English drama and to a style of furniture – Jacobean. There was no spectacular change from Elizabethan to Jacobean furniture styles – both, indeed, might be regarded as English Renaissance – but because the early New England and Virginia colonists had come to maturity in the reign of King James, they tended to carry over either the actual furniture of that time or the models of such in their minds and tastes.

It is probably almost universal and inevitable that the English who settled in America during the seventeenth century tended to hold to this familiar Jacobean style long after the time when their kinfolk back in England were moving on to new styles. So the furniture of the English in America until the late 1600s tends to be somewhat 'blocky'– mainly straight elements and joints at right angles. There are moldings and turnings and carvings, to be sure, but they are relatively simple. There are exceptions, but they are just that – extraordinary pieces that were probably saved by generations of descendents precisely because they were so striking.

One of the most common pieces of furniture, one that all classes of the English colonists found necessary and that therefore has survived in considerable numbers, was the chest. This was used for storing household textiles and at least some clothes and personal possessions, and considering that few people could afford many other storage pieces and that most houses must have been rather smoky and dirty, such chests were an absolute necessity. Some chests must have been brought over from England (although one that was long believed to have been brought over on the *Mayflower* by Edward Winslow is now thought, due to its wood, to have been made in New England) but in any case the colonists had many and clear models in mind. The basic type of construction was one of a joined frame with inset panels, but there were a number of variations on this, and the English in New England, although some continued making traditional types long after they had gone out of fashion in England, often tried new forms.

Thus, because large trees were so plentiful in the New England forests, the English settlers could afford to have long and wide boards cut and then make chests by nailing these lengthwise – a cheaper method than the traditional joined frame-and-panels. Or the colonists felt free to lavish considerable time and talent in decorating their chests – sometimes with quite intricate carvings, sometimes with spindles, bosses and other turnings and moldings, and more often than not with various bright colors of paint. The tops, sides and backs were usually left plain, but the fronts were ornamented in quite varied and even dazzling ways.

The chests of the seventeenth-century English colonists also developed along other lines. By 1650, chests with a drawer at the bottom were being made in Massachusetts – although the drawer had been known in Europe long before this, this represents a significant advance in craftsmanship for colonists. Since these drawers were quite large and heavy – there are bottoms made of 50-inch-wide and one-inch thick oak boards – they would usually be supported by a center runner that was slotted so as to run along a channel. Shortly after chests with single drawers began to appear, chests with two ranks of drawers were also being made in New England, and then chests with three or more ranks of drawers. There is a superb example dated at 1678 and attributed to either William Searle or his successor, Thomas Dennis, of Newbury, Massachusetts. By this time the old, simple chests may be thought of as

This carved chest, attributed to Thomas Dennis of Newbury, Massachusetts, still shows traces of the original paint.

having evolved into an essentially new type of furniture, a chest of drawers.

Simultaneously with these developments – and it should not be thought that furniture 'evolved' in some linear, progressive fashion, discarding 'obsolete' forms: if anything, new forms just kept being added to previous ones – there were several special variants on the traditional chest in America. In the area of Hartford and Wethersfield, Connecticut, for instance, in the late decades of the seventeenth century, chests – usually with two ranks of drawers – were being decorated with distinctive sunflower and tulip carvings (and sometimes asters). Such motifs can be traced back to earlier English and Scottish traditions, but this 'school' seems to have thrived in this one section of Connecticut. Meanwhile, only about 50 miles north, along the Connecticut River, in an area that seems to have centered around Hadley, Massachusetts, a similar 'school' of chest-ornamentation was thriving. The so-called Hadley chests, however, had virtually their entire fronts carved with flower, leaf, vine and other motifs – and these in turn were usually painted in various colors; the Hadley chests also usually had the owner's name or initials and a date carved on the front – suggesting they were used as 'dower chests' (that is, used by young women to gather linens and other belongings that would go with them as part of their dowry when they married). And still later in the century, around Guilford, Connecticut, still another school of chest decoration emerged, with painted designs based on old English or Dutch motifs.

As the American colonists began to settle in and acquire more possessions, they had to store an increasing variety of objects, both household and personal, and so they began to construct a variety of chests and cupboards. Open cupboards were something of a status symbol. One could just as well put glassware or pewter or whatever inside closed spaces, but if one could afford the space for a cupboard and leave some of the finer objects on display, this gave some sense of economic and social standing. There were two basic types of cupboards: one that was open on the top but enclosed below was known as a press cupboard, while another which had its enclosed section over an open lower section was known as a court cupboard (from the French, *court*, for short, or low). Some of these cupboards became quite elaborate in their structural and ornamental details.

Storing textiles – again, even the homes of the well-to-do during the seventeenth century must have been rather smoky – presented a special challenge. Few houses anywhere in the world at this time had built-in cupboards or closets (still true in large parts of the world) so people had long been using freestanding closets, or wardrobes. Each ethnic or national group of colonists tended to bring over to the New World the name and type of wardrobe they had grown up with: for the French, this was an *armoire*; for the Dutch, a *kas*; for the Germans, a *schrank*; for the English, the standard name for such a wardrobe was a 'press,' or 'linen press.' Naturally, there was some variation in these large wardrobes from national group to national group and from age to age and class to class, but the surprising fact is that there was so little variation; some might have a drawer on the bottom, some might have more elaborate feet or top, but all were essentially two-door cupboards.

A two drawer 'Hadley' chest with the overall shallow carving which is typical of that area of the upper Connecticut River Valley.

Furniture from Guilford or Saybrook Connecticut was frequently elaborately painted, as is this five-drawer chest.

Where there was variation, however, was in the ornamentation, or decorative elements. For the poorer families, plain board might do, but as families prospered they were able to indulge in quite elaborate wardrobes, with intricate

carvings, inlaid panels, turned elements, expensive woods, and – at least in the case of the Dutch and Germans – colorful painted surfaces. Such wardrobes served both a necessary function and again as something of a status symbol, at the same time linking people to their cultural traditions.

Another necessary piece of furniture was a bed, although in the poorer families people slept on little more than mattresses on the ground. A 'bed', in fact, to seventeenth-century English actually referred to the mattress, not to the wooden frame; this was called a 'bedstead' (the 'bed place' as in 'homestead'). These wooden bedsteads tended to be one of four basic types. There were the light frames made of turned elements and joined by simple horizontal elements; there were those that had headboards – often quite elaborate – joined by horizontals to turned front posts; there were the trundle beds, very low and simple frames that had wheels, or casters, under the four legs so that they could be easily rolled under a larger bed during the day; and finally there were the bedsteads with high posts and sometimes overhead frames called 'testers', which supported all kinds of textile hangings, often extremely elaborate and expensive. (These are now known as 'tester beds' or familiarly as 'fourposters.')

Tables were another basic piece of furniture, but here the limitations of space in most seventeenth-century colonists' houses became the governing factor. Most of the daily activities took place in the one main downstairs room, the 'hall,' and when one considers the size of families, the variety of jobs performed by each family (from farming to clothes making), the fact that most cooking was done at an open fire at one end of the main hall – it is no wonder that most of the early settlers had to be satisfied with one table and that even this one, if possible, might be with either knockdown or folding elements. Thus, long trestle tables were made with a flat top board that could be lifted off the

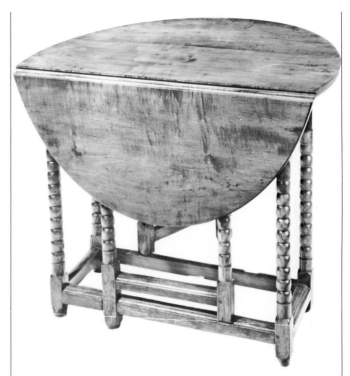

A gate-leg table with two drop leaves could be stored against the wall.

two or three trestle supports; these in turn were held together by a horizontal 'stretcher' that was attached to the trestles by removable wooden pins, or pegs. A braced, or sawbuck, table was similar, with a crossrail held to the braces by wedges. Such knockdown tables could be easily taken apart and stored to one side of a room. Meanwhile, there were several types of folding tables – most with gate-legs that pivoted out to support the leaves. The

The top of this trestle table is easily removed, and the stretchers taken apart for storage. These tables could be set up for each meal and taken down afterward.

earliest known English gate-legs tables go back to the fifteenth century and were oval or semi-circular and had only one leaf which folded down onto the top when not in use. The type of gate-leg table that had two side leaves hanging down from the fixed center board did not appear in England until the early seventeenth century, but the English colonists were soon making their own.

This need to clear as much usable space as possible went far back before the English colonists settle in the New World, and from the Middle Ages there were a variety of folding and collapsible and double-duty items of furniture. In addition to the tables that could be folded or disassembled, there were folding beds and combination chair-tables – the latter also sometimes having a drawer beneath the seat to provide much-needed, if small, storage space. One quite special solution to the space problem was the draw table, with a mechanism beneath the top that allowed flat leaves to be drawn forth at both ends and thus extend the length of the table when needed for large gatherings. (Only one such draw table is known from seventeenth-century America.)

But it was in the making of chairs that the English colonists seem to have exercised the most ingenuity. Poorer people actually may often have done without chairs – after all, they could just as well sit on blocks of wood or barrels or stools, and there were also 'forms,' or what we would call benches, still used wherever people wanted to sit down in a more communal or shared occasion (a church supper, a sporting event). A chair, indeed, had once denoted some special status, whether a throne or the 'chair-man of the board' (that is, as opposed to those who sat around a table on stools or benches). It is no coincidence, then, that among the oldest surviving pieces of furniture from New England are chairs that are claimed to have been owned by several of the most prominent elders of the colonies. These 'great chayers' include: the Carver Chair, which tradition claims belonged to Governor John Carver of the Plymouth Colony and is now considered to have been made in England; the Bradford Chair, said to have belonged to Governor William Bradford, author of the famous *History of Plimoth Plantation* – a more elaborate version of the Carver Chair; the Brewster Chair – much like the Bradford Chair, but the possession of William Brewster; the

The press cupboard has a closed lower section. The elaborate carvings are typical of the English Jacobean style.

Winslow Chair, a quite different type of chair than the previous three – they being made of turned parts, the Winslow Chair being made by joined pieces, including a back panel; and the Endicott Chair, the possession of Dr Zerrubabel Endicott of Salem, Massachusetts, and unique in being the only upholstered armchair known to have survived from seventeenth century New England – the covering being leather.

These are special chairs, to be sure, in that they belonged to notables and have survived, but they should not be regarded as one-of-a-kind. Many chairs of exactly these types were made in the New England colonies – some with such similar turnings that they can be traced to individual chair-makers. Even the leather-upholstered Endicott Chair, as exceptional as it is as a survivor, was probably not unique in its day, certainly not in England. This Endicott Chair is covered in Russian leather that had been imported via England; the original leather survives, as do most of the original shiny brass-headed nails. By the end of the seventeenth century, Boston was noted for its production of leather-covered chairs, which were soon being

exported throughout much of North America and even down to the Caribbean.

Yet another type of chair made in the English colonies of New England was the wainscot armchair. This name requires some defining as 'wainscot' today refers to the wood paneling that extends around the bottom 3-4 feet of a wall; originally, however, *wain* was an old Germanic word for 'wagon' while *schot* was the 'crossbar' or 'partition' – so that a 'wainscot' referred to the wooden panel, probably made of the finest oak, and possibly carved with some care; eventually the term 'wainscot' came to be applied to a chair – traditionally made of oak – with a broad paneled back carved (or sometimes inlaid), often with quite extravagant 'gothic' designs. The chair itself is typically very

Left: *The chair-table could be used two ways. It also has a drawer for storage, under the seat.*
Below: *The John Alden Family Great Chair.*

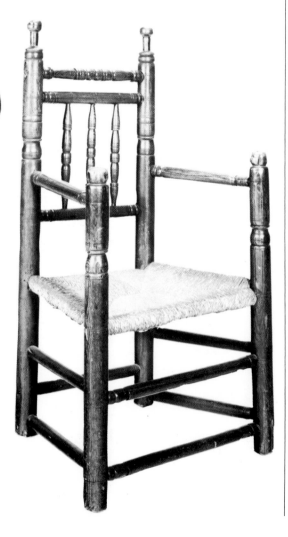

sturdy, foursquare and imposing, with prominent arms that seem to exude authority, and it seems to be a direct descendent of medieval chairs associated with the great barons and the clerical hierarchy. There are several truly stunning such wainscot chairs that have survived from seventeenth-century New England, one by William Searle, a joiner from Ipswich, Massachusetts, and a second by Thomas Dennis, who worked for Searle and then married his widow: both men came from Ottery-St-Mary in the west of England, where this style of woodcarving was traditional – although Searle's carving, in particular, is considered to be superior to most of that done in England.

One thing that should be apparent by now is that the New England colonists did not seem to be living up to their reputation as dour, drab Puritans, skulking about in black and opposed to all forms of color, ornamentation and pleasure. (In fact it was only the ministers who went

The arm chair of Dr Zerrubabel Endicott of Salem is upholstered in the original leather. The cushion is modern.

The wainscot-armchair, designed and carved by Thomas Dennis, has elements typical of the English West Country.

about always in black clothes.) To be sure, in their religious life they practiced great constraint, but in the privacy of their homes these seventeenth-century New Englanders seem to have been open to considerable variety in their furniture. Perhaps it was the influence of the craftsmen, the furniture-makers themselves, who after the first difficult years must have been anxious to show what they could do. The first generation or two of furniture-makers in the New England colonies, after all, were immigrants from England or other European lands, and they had longstanding traditions of technique and style to draw on. Meanwhile the colonists were moving ahead and must have wanted some tangible signs of their pride and prosperity. (The early wills of these New Englanders reveal that they had many fine pieces of furniture to pass on.)

In any case, whether the impulse came from the craftsmen or from the prospering citizenry, the furniture of these seventeenth-century New Englanders was soon being decorated in ways that belie the reputation of the Puritans and their 'plain style.' Carving, turning, painting, inlay, all these techniques were used quite early on. We have already noted a number of pieces of furniture that required the mastery of some of these techniques – the superb carved chair by Searle (and he is credited with other equally sophisticated items), the fine turned 'great chayers' prized by the notables, the painted

Below: A seventeenth-century child's high chair has a wooden seat and turned spindles.

chests of Connecticut, the inlaid work on chests and cupboards. Some of these pieces were fashioned by anonymous joiners – still the basic word for furniture-makers – and turners, but the skill required to prepare the various parts and then put them together using the mortise-and-tenon method, so that a piece that was both durable and handsome resulted – this was no mean achievement.

The myth of New Englanders' total aversion to color and material possessions, let alone anything suggesting opulence, is nowhere more belied than in the fine textiles used for beds or in the upholstery work. Not many of the original textiles have survived, but inventories and wills of the period attest to the value placed on the 'hangings' used with tester beds. And although upholstered furniture was not to become all that common until the eighteenth century, there were some upholstered pieces being made in New England during the last half of the seventeenth century. There are even two fine upholstered couches that survive from seventeenth-century New England. The one in the Essex Institute is covered with so-called turkey work: quite brilliant shades of red, blue, and yellow wool yarn were woven on a coarse canvas in geometric patterns to imitate hand-knotted carpets made in Turkey (or elsewhere in the Middle East). Such turkey-work fabric was made in England and used widely for table covers and bed hangings.

Another factor or force at work would lead the American colonists into increasingly diversified and thus innovative styles of furniture was what might be called 'regionalism.' Even within the New England colonies, as we have already seen, and with just one simple type such as chests, there would be considerable variety – from Guilford, Connecticut, Hartford-Wethersfield, Connecticut, to the Hadley, Massachusetts, area. And there are still other distinct sub-variants, recognizable to experts at least, such as the Taunton chest or the Dedham chest. Locales such as the North Shore above Boston – Ipswich, Salem, and such – or New Haven, Connecticut, not to mention a major center such as Boston, soon began to put a distinctive imprint on their furniture (and on virtually all their other possessions, such as glass, silver and ceramics).

Right: Bright embroidery or turkey work was frequently used to upholster furniture in the seventeenth century.

The upholstered couch was a luxury in the seventeenth century. The frame of this one is oak and maple.

But undoubtedly the major influence on the diversity of the total American experience stemmed from the different colonies that took hold in regions quite removed from New England, colonies founded by people of different national-ethnic traditions that would inevitably be expressed in their material culture such as furniture. For that matter, even the English colonies of Virginia and the South – around Chesapeake Bay and down into the Carolinas – differed noticeably from those of New England. Those in Virginia had taken hold before Plymouth and Boston, of course, but they were founded by people with different motives and goals: simplistically stated, the Virginia English were there for economic, not religious reasons. (The Anglican Church, for instance, was supported in Virginia: the oldest surviving church structure in the English colonies, for example, is St. Luke's in Smithfield, Virginia – 1632 – and it is almost a perfect example of a small English medieval parish church.) The Virginia colonists, and those of nearby Southern areas in general, were not there to establish 'a city on a hill' as the Boston Puritans saw their mission but to take advantage of the fine climate and rich land. Jamestown, in fact, was to be a satellite of the commercial center of London, and light industries were originally planned – glassworks, potteries, ironworks, wine presses, carpenters' shops – but the colonists soon discovered that the easiest money could be made from cash crops, particularly tobacco. Eventually other cash crops were added – rice and indigo, for instance – and soon large plantations were spreading across the land, all too soon to be worked by black slaves.

What effect did this have on the furniture of these Southern colonists? Almost from the beginning, they started dealing directly with London as their main source of supply for material goods of all kinds, for that was where they sold their own produce. This meant that the Southerners found it convenient to buy their household furnishings of all kinds in London. As the New England colonies began to make furniture, the Southerners also began to purchase their furniture there (and also from other Northern colonies in New York,

An early seventeenth-century cupboard from Virginia is identifiable by the open display shelf.

Pennsylvania, etc). Then, too, as the Southern colonists began to operate within a commercial network that did not expect dedication to a single religious-communal ideal, they were ready to bring over craftsmen of different nationalities – Dutch, French, German, Italian, Polish, even Persian. All this led to its own peculiar combination of conservatism and diversity within these Southern colonists: prosperous plantation owners would continue to furnish their fine homes with furniture bought in London or Boston while in the small towns and countryside the poorer folk were left to buy theirs from less skillful itinerant carpenters. The result is that relatively few pieces of American-made furniture from the seventeenth century have survived in the South, although there are several notable pieces such as a court cupboard from eastern Virginia (an almost straight replica of an Elizabethan English type) or the wardrobe, or press, also from eastern Virginia, that has the unusual feature of one door being narrower than the other, and with shelves behind the narrow door.

It is in such idiosyncrasies that the spirit of Southern furniture of this century most commonly expresses itself.

In terms of sheer seniority, of course, it should be the furniture of the Spanish colonies that is the oldest and most distinguished. The Spaniards, after all, were the first Europeans to explore and settle the Americas and by 1600 it must have appeared that the New World was going to be a branch of Spain. But this was not to be, and the same reasons that are familiar from American history in general explain why furniture does not survive from the Spanish colonies in North America. Again, simplistically put, the Spanish came seeking glory, gold and souls, and they were not particularly interested in bringing over the colonists and craftsmen who would call for fine furniture. Even the areas where the Spanish tended to settle – the South and Southwest – tended to be poor in the woods required for fine furniture; the Southwest, for instance, provided such coarse woods as cottonwood, juniper, piñon, red spruce, and Western yellow pine. Meanwhile, although some priests, soldiers, and administrators may have possessed a few skills

Left: A press cupboard with drawers below was used for storage of linen and clothes.

or a bit of knowledge relevant to furniture-making, the Spaniards generally just put the local Indians to making imitations of familiar furniture. The resultant work was inevitably rather crude, even degenerate in the technical sense: the Spanish styles and motifs were seen by the Indians through their own perceptive modes and then they tried to adapt or impose their own forms – which happened to involve more geometric and abstract elements, for instance – so that the end result was furniture that was neither fish nor fowl, neither Spanish nor Indian. In any case, little of North American-Spanish furniture from before 1700 has survived. It is perhaps no coincidence that when the Arts and Crafts movement emerged in the late nineteenth century, with its aim of casting off the 'artificial' European layers that had accrued to furniture, one of the more natural styles revived was that of the Spanish Southwest. To that extent, the Spaniards and Indians would gain some standing in the history of American furniture.

If the Spanish seemed to be the dominant force in North America by 1600, it was the French who must have appeared so by 1700. At home, the French were more populous than the English, for instance, and they had the most stable government; France was probably the strongest nation in Europe, in fact. Meanwhile, from Quebec and along the St Lawrence Valley, down the Mississippi, along the Atlantic Seaboard from Canada to Florida, the French had a network of settlements trading posts, and forts. But just as with the Spanish, the reasons that are now generally accepted as explaining France's role in North America also affect the furniture from the French communities in North America. Like the Spanish, the French sent administrators, troops, and missionaries with the idea of exploiting a commercial colony of native Americans rather than sending large numbers of French colonists. The result can be seen in the two tracks taken by the furniture from the French communities in North America. The upper classes, generally living in a few large towns or cities, tended to be conservative and retained their Old World traditions even longer than did the English. Their houses and public buildings, for instance, were apt to be replicas of French structures. So too did the so-called town style of French-American furniture tend to reflect the high styles of France: seventeenth-century French-

American furniture-makers imitated the sequence of styles then current in *La Belle France* – Louis Treize, Renaissance, Louis Quatorze. The other track was that of the rural communities, the so-called habitant style; it was not unexpectedly utilitarian in its conception, sturdy in its construction, and rather naive in its decorative elements. This habitant style often harks back directly to the Gothic-medieval traditions of French furniture, and now appears to be close to folk art in its simple colors and patterns. But it must also be recognized that the two styles, town and habitant, were not always kept absolutely separate; there are pieces of furniture that combine elements of both. And both, after all, share an underlying conservatism. Thus, the oak tree did not grow so well in the northern regions of New France, so the French-Canadians would substitute local woods such as pine, walnut, cherry or wild cherry; but the furniture-makers still tended to carve and shape these softer, more malleable woods with the forms they had previously been forced to shape in the less tractable oak. Such conservatism, of course, is by no means peculiar to French-American craftsmen but can be found throughout history.

There was another group of French who did have a more direct impact on the mainstream developments of furniture in North America – the Huguenots, or French Protestants. After the terrible persecutions and struggles of the sixteenth century, French Protestants had in 1598 been granted at least some toleration by the Edict of Nantes issued by Henry IV. During the seventeenth century, however, these Huguenots began to lose their political freedoms within predominantly Roman Catholic society. In 1628, for instance, a royal decree prohibited Protestants from settling in any colony in New France (North America). What this meant, though, was that the Huguenots began to go to the English and other colonies in the New World – South Carolina, Massachusetts, New York. (By 1680, for instance, one-quarter of New York City's population was Huguenot.) Then in 1685, Louis XIV repealed the Edict of Nantes; thousands of Huguenots fled to Holland, England, Prussia and America. (By 1750, some

Left: *By the end of the century, luxuries like paneling, brick hearths, firebacks and carpets were available in the colonies. (The Thomas Hart House Parlor, Metropolitan Museum of Art, New York)*

15,000 Huguenots had immigrated into the English colonies of North America; one such was Apollos Revere, whose son Paul was to play an influential role in the birth of the United States.)

But the relevant point about these Huguenot emigrants is that they were generally a prosperous group, many of them skilled craftsmen, particularly in the making of textiles. Some of these Huguenots had a direct influence on English and Dutch furniture-making during the seventeenth century and then, when this furniture or actual Huguenots arrived in the American colonies, on American furniture.

Another group that had a somewhat similar history in Europe and that was to make a distinctive contribution to American furniture were the German Protestants who also emigrated to the New World to escape persecution. Since most came from the Palatinate in southwestern Germany, they were often known as 'Palatines'; once settled in Pennsylvania, where they concentrated, they were known by their own name for 'German,' *Deutsch*, but this got turned into 'Dutch' – thus the now well-known Pennsylvania Dutch. They first settled in Germantown (on the edge of Philadelphia) at the end of the seventeenth century but they did not come in great numbers until after 1720, and then they spread throughout the counties of eastern Pennsylvania. These Pennsylvania Dutch brought with them familiar types of furniture, (folk art, a commitment to craftsmanship, and a dedication to their old traditions); the result was to be a quite distinctive school of furniture that would only begin to take hold at the end of the seventeenth century. It would be noted for several types of furniture such as dower chests and slat-backed chairs and the large *schranks*, or wardrobes, but most of all this Pennsylvania Dutch tradition would be marked by its painted decorations.

The other main group that was to contribute its distinctive heritage to seventeenth-century America were the Dutch, who during the first half of the century settled not only in New Amsterdam on Manhattan Island but up the Hudson Valley to Albany and Schenectady, eastward onto Long Island, and westward into New Jersey and the Delaware River. Like several of the other European communities, the Dutch were originally interested in commerce, not colonization; like other groups, too, their

settlers tended to split into two groups – the prosperous burghers, or urban merchants, and the patroons, or great landowners, forming one, the poorer laborers and farmers forming the other – that maintained two types of furniture. The prosperous Dutch could afford to import furnishings of all kinds – pictures, ceramics, textiles, furniture – and in any case wanted furniture that kept up with the best in contemporary style; the poorer and rural Dutch had to be content with simpler, almost folk-style

Hanging cupboards and chests for storing earthenware, horn, and pewter plates and utensils were found in most houses. (Winterthur)

furniture – chairs, for instance, that were decidedly unelegant, with leather seats and triangular blocks supporting their legs and joints. But one item of furniture that all the Dutch seem to have owned was the *kas*, or wardrobe; this had a long tradition in the Netherlands, of course, and was not brought over to the New World until the second half of the seventeenth century, but then it took hold and was kept alive well into the nineteenth century. There were two main types: those with painted surfaces – often highly ornate and with *trompe l'oeil*; and those with woodwork – panels, inlay, grooves, often almost architectural in effect and in a baroque manner. Unlike the presses of the English, the *armoires* of the French or the *schranks* of the Germans, many of the Dutch *kasten* had interiors decorated with

The Dutch colonists in the Hudson River Valley decorated their presses called kasten *with elaborate* trompe l'oeil *painting.*

tiles or ceramics, textiles, or even brass or copper. Clearly the Dutch of all classes regarded a *kas* as both a basic necessity and as a symbol of identification.

In 1664, England took over the colony of New Netherlands, and New Amsterdam became New York, but the joiners and turners who had been making furniture in the Dutch tradition just went on working. For almost from the beginning, New Amsterdam had been a relatively cosmopolitan settlement, welcoming people from countries in Europe besides the Netherlands, from other colonies along the the Atlantic Coast, and even from the West Indies. New

Englanders, who had started out with some sense of needing to stay apart to fulfill their destiny, also began to deal with the merchants of New Amsterdam, and by the last quarter of the seventeenth century there was considerable exchange among New England and the other colonies. By this time, some 100,000 Englishmen alone had immigrated into the New World and there was a new spirit that was beginning to be felt in the American colonies. Partly it came about from the sheer passage of time, the acclimatization, so to speak, of former Europeans and immigrants to the new American environment and society; partly it came about from new demands and new prosperity of all classes, but particularly those of the growing merchant and urban communities. Put another way, more people from more backgounds now had more time and more money to want more things – including furniture.

This thrust of events in the American Colonies coincided with developments in Europe, where again, the simple passage of time was generating advances in learning, science, and taste. But in particular, England was going through quite a major change: Charles II was restored to the throne after having spent many years on the Continent where he was exposed to the cultures of France and the Netherlands. He also acquired a Portuguese princess, Catherine of Braganza, as a wife. The court of Charles II began to introduce a far more cosmopolitan culture to England, including more sophisticated furniture, and by the last three decades or so of the century such developments were spreading to the American Colonies.

Some of the changes can be directly traced to events in England and in Europe: for instance, the flight of Protestants such as the Huguenots of France and those of the German Palatinate and Low Countries, many of whom were skilled craftsmen – specifically furnituremakers who settled in England, where they introduced new techniques and types to English furnituremakers. Other changes seem a bit more tenuous: for instance, King Charles II's Portuguese wife is sometimes said to have brought about the new type of chair with arched or pierced stretchers that was called the 'Portuguese style.'

Other changes in furnituremaking came about probably because it is simply in the nature of any discipline to develop and refine its techniques with the passage of time. Thus the basic method of English furnituremaking for centuries, was the mortise-and-tenon with the peg. But now, in the last half of the seventeenth century, English furnituremakers began to use a new method, one that employed a fitted dovetail to frame chests, drawers and other elements. This new method meant that, instead of constantly relying on heavy oak for frames and panels, furnituremakers could employ lighter, thinner woods. And this lightness was more than just a matter of weight; it meant more flexible shapes in both the design and function of furniture; this in turn led to more elegant and more sophisticated types of furniture and ornamentatation. It also led to the introduction of a new name for furnituremakers – 'cabinetmakers,' a word that begins to come into use in England and the American colonies only in the last decades of the seventeenth century.

This change in the name of an occupation might not at first seem that important but it signifies a major shift from the methods and associations of medieval joinery: it is no coincidence, for instance, that most pieces of furniture in seventeenth-century America are by anonymous joiners, while in the eighteenth century cabinetmakers will begin to sign and label their works. Meanwhile, the new flexibility and elegance that emerged with the new dovetail method also prompted the adoption of other new techniques. Glue began to be used for applying veneer, which allowed for increasingly more exotic woods that were placed over such basic woods as pine. There will be new forms of ornamentation – deeper turnings, scroll carvings, more elaborate inlay work, the type known as marquetry.

The American Colonies, then, although lagging behind England and other European countries, were on the verge of trying new types of furniture by the last decade of the seventeenth century. Through the increasing contacts among the various national and ethnic groups that had settled in the New World and because of the breakdown of some of the age-old structures and distinctions in social classes, the American colonists were well situated to take their furniture in new directions. And Americans, although by no means inventing new types of furniture at this stage, would be as quick as any people to adopt and adapt forms and techniques. The American experience was truly being reflected in American furniture.

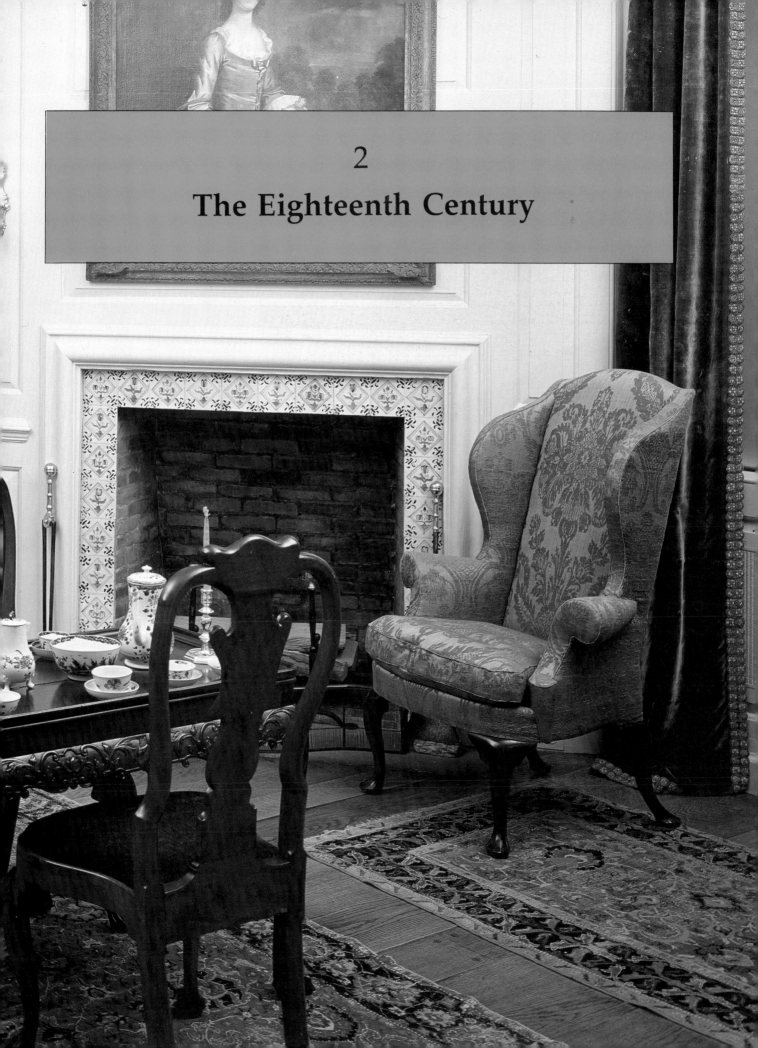

2
The Eighteenth Century

By 1700 English civilization had become firmly planted in North America. The twelve established colonies had a population over 220,000. The country was growing at such a pace that those figures doubled every twenty years. Villages were becoming towns and a few towns were taking on the airs of cities. The people living in them had ceased to think of themselves as transplanted Englishmen or Scots or Dutchmen and were beginning to acquire attitudes and tastes that were uniquely American.

With more settled living patterns evolving and the labor force growing, the colonies could support for the first time a host of true craft industries employing fulltime professionals. Furniture-making was one of the first and most vigorous craft specialities to evolve in the new century.

Several factors lay behind this development. Probably the most significant was the matter of utility. There was a real need for chairs, tables, cabinets and other household furnishings that

Previous page: Rich merchants and landowners in the eighteenth century imported Dutch tiles and Oriental rugs to enhance their parlors and drawing rooms. (The Readbourne Parlor at Winterthur)

Above: Sidechairs upholstered in leather, and decorated with brass nail heads, became more common in the late seventeenth century.

could not yet be said to exist for paintings, sculpture or even formal architecture. Paired with this, there was a growing class of prosperous patrons eager to display their wealth and taste and to enjoy the amenities of a more comfortable domestic life. For the first time, a skilled artisan could find a market for his wares beyond the narrow precincts of his neighborhood. He could develop more specialized skills, too, and in so doing separate himself from the ranks of the carpenter-joiners who built houses and boats and farm tools as well as simple furniture.

Those colonists in a position to do so responded to the growing sophistication of native craftsmen by buying American work, as evidenced by the dramatic reduction in foreign-made goods in the beginning of the eighteenth century. Between 1697 and 1704, for example, Americans imported from England £18,184 in cabinets and case goods, and £47,441 in upholstered pieces, for a total of £65,625 worth of furniture. In the same span of years some twenty years later, they brought in a mere £8,328 worth of foreign-made cabinets and seating. Considering that the population continued to soar, and with it the need for household goods, this change of affections becomes even more dramatic.

Stylistically, art historians like to define the evolution of eighteenth-century American furniture-making in terms of four progressive styles. Traditionally, these styles are termed William and Mary, c 1690-c 1725; Queen Anne, c 1725-c 1750; Chippendale, c 1750-c 1785; and Federal, c 1785-c 1820. It is interesting to note here that in each instance the American style mirrors to a significant degree the same changes taking place in England, though the changes come ten to twenty-five years later. It is well to remember that early furniture history is, by its nature, an inexact science. Eighteenth-century American pieces were rarely dated or signed, and because furniture is relatively portable, even the place of origin can be difficult to determine.

The last decades of the seventeenth century were a time of great expansiveness in the Colonies. As in England, the heavy yoke of the Commonwealth had been lifted. Though Americans were not to feel the social and artistic changes as soon or as fully as the English, still the restoration of the monarchy had inspired a certain way of living in England that inevitably raised the sights of many colonials as well. With each passing season, with each new shipment of fancy silks and china, of fine wigs and architects' pattern books, Americans could not help but be influenced to alter the trappings of their households and their lives.

The first period, marked by the adoption of the William and Mary style, takes its name from Prince William of Orange and his English wife Mary who crossed the Channel in 1688 to assume the British throne jointly after Mary's father, King James II, had been exiled to France. Their reign became a conduit for the importation of Continental tastes in architecture and the decorative arts. Dutch as well as French Huguenot artists and craftsmen were much sought after not only by the royal household but by all who could afford their services. From Britain's Anglo-Dutch court to the royal governors' palaces of the Colonies to the domestic hearths of prosperous subjects up and down the Atlantic coast, the new mode moved with deliberate speed, bringing changes both in interior architecture and furniture.

In American houses built after the turn of the century there was a visible change in the scale of the interiors, with the heights and sizes of rooms typically increased. The simply-sheathed walls that had been satisfactory in a plainer time, were replaced with wainscoted walls and raised panels. Sash windows came into general use. Walls were often painted, too. Furniture of the William and Mary period was notably different in many ways from the medieval Jacobean style that it supplanted. Instead of the massive, rectilinear forms, the heavy carving and vigorous strapwork, the bulbous turnings, that characterized the earlier style, the new furniture was lighter, the carving more restrained. Instead of a preponderance of coarse-grained oak, the new pieces were often of finer-grained wood. Maple, cherry, and walnut were especially popular. Surfaces of the new furniture were sometimes decorated with costly veneers and inlays, the sophisticated techniques for which were directly traceable to the Dutch and French. A taste for 'China worke' – in the form of lacquered surfaces, gilding and caning – was another distinguishing feature of this period. And what had been a fairly narrow range of furniture types – straight chairs, basic chests and cupboards, bedsteads and tables constituting the essential furniture ensemble of virtually all households – was now being expanded to include an extremely wide variety of specialty pieces.

Changes that appear in the design of seats at this time included a tendency to greater variety in style and size, more emphasis on comfort. Most notable, it was during this period that the upholstered wing chair made its first appearance. The wing chair is descended from the English 'sleeping chayer', a short-lived conceit of Restoration design. A species of daybed, this piece featured an iron ratchet mechanism that made it possible to crank one end of the couch up to a sitting position, thereby converting it to a chair. Its other features – a frame that was covered with cushioning and padding and 'wings' that projected forward from the movable chairbed back – made it not only more accommodating to the human form but also wonderfully protective against cold drafts. The ratchet was soon abandoned as more trouble that it was worth, and the upright wing chair, called an 'easy chair' by Jacobean Englishmen, adopted.

The typical upholstered easy chair as it appeared in the Colonies during the William and Mary era featured a tall back, arms that rolled outward horizontally, and front legs that ended in a type of carving known as 'the Spanish foot'. This detail, which consisted of a tapering scrolled motif, had its stylistic origins in Portugal and was apparently introduced to England by Catherine of Braganza, the queen of Charles II (1660-1685).

Chairs without upholstery tended to be more comfortable than their predecessors, too, thanks in part to the use of caning for more resilient backs and seats. (Cane, or rattan which was woven from the trailing vines of a species of East Indian climbing palm, was introduced to the West by the Dutch and Portuguese. A vogue for its use in furniture arose in England during the late 1600s and reached the Colonies soon after.) Leather, which had become a favored upholstery material for the Cromwell chairs of the previous century, continued to be used as well. Rush, woven seating made from the fibrous stems and leaves of the common rush plant, remained a thrifty alternative to other seat materials as it had been in previous furniture periods.

As for the general proportions, turning, and carving details of all-wood chairs, William and Mary pieces are characterized by more slender

An early Easy Chair, which belonged to Benjamin Franklin's cousin, has an elaborate scalloped apron and a down-filled cushion.

lines, taller backs, and more varied ornamentation than was seen during the previous period. Pierced crests adorned many of the finer pieces, which might also include vertical banister backs or horizontal slat backs. Arms, when they were included, now were often contoured rather than straight, showing yet another accommodation to human comfort and visual elegance. Stretchers were usually plain or nearly so on the sides and rear, turned with finesse at the front. Legs, especially front legs, often showed ornamental turning, Spanish scrolled or bulbous feet.

A specialized chair for which American colonists seem to have had a special fondness was the corner chair, alternatively known as the roundabout or writing chair. Used for sitting at the card table or desk, its wide-angled continuous arm and back design was designed to accommodate the flaring coats and extravagantly wide skirts fashionable in this period.

The design of the corner chair was especially practical when women wore full skirts.

Chairs were not the only category of furniture whose invention is traceable to the activity of writing; the notion of desks also entered the American Colonies during the William and Mary era. Bible boxes or 'scholar's boxes', which were portable wooden cases furnished with writing materials, had been around for some time, but in the first decades of the eighteenth century they assumed the scale and importance of full-sized, floor-standing pieces. (Historians take this development as a sure indication of the growing literacy of the population and the important role letter-writing played in the social and economic commerce of the new country; by 1690 the colonists had their own Deputy Postmaster and more or less regular postal delivery service between Portsmouth, New Hampshire and Philadelphia.)

Three types of desks became conventional: the desk-on-frame, the slope-front desk, and the desk-with-bookcase or secretary. The desk-on-frame was in effect a scholar's box on legs. The earliest examples were hinged at the top to lift upward, giving access to writing materials inside. To write at the desk, however, one had to stand and work atop the closed lid. Later

The flap of a slant-front desk folds down to make a writing surface and reveal the drawers and cupboards behind. The fan carving was very popular.

examples put the hinges at the bottom and added pull-out slides so that the slanted lid could rest in an open postion. The writer could then do his writing and figuring while comfortably seated. A separate drawer, inserted in the panel that held the slides, was another added nicety. Slides, which were at first rather crude and squarish in cross-section, gradually became more slender and graceful, too.

The slope-front desk was a still greater refinement in writing furniture. Where its predecessor was supported by a table, the slope-front desk rested on a chest of drawers and offered considerably more storage. Not surprisingly, it soon replaced the desk-on-frame as the preferred design.

The fall-front desk was a more massive, architecturally-impressive, version of the slope-front. Here when the desk was not being used, the lid closed in an upright position against the face of the cabinet, as if it were a panelled door. Several tiers of drawers and cubby/holes were hidden behind the lid which, because of its greater size and weight, required folding hangers to support it when dropped. The usual complement of chest drawers were provided beneath. The last variant, the desk-with-bookcase or secretary, typically combined a slant-topped desk with provisions for shelving books in a two-doored cabinet above.

Drawer handles on all kinds of desks in this period were typically tear-drop pulls with small circular or diamond-shaped backplates, all cast in brass. (Cast brass had supplanted wrought iron handles in the late seventeenth century.) Hinges might be simple iron butterfly hinges or ornamental brass. Many desk lids featured locks, another sign that Colonists took their writing seriously. Virtually all the fancy hardware was imported from England.

The dressing table was another speciality piece of furniture that first appeared in the William and Mary era. Dubbed a lowboy at a much later date, the dressing table was intended as the locus of the lady's toilet. Pomades, lip salves, powders, rouges, brushes and combs, and other toiletries were to be stored in the three or more drawers provided across the front of the piece. A skirt or apron, with an arched central portion, not only served as a focal point for the piece but provided a kneehole so that the owner could sit in comfort as she worked. An easel mirror, together with jewel boxes, a hair receiver, and candle sticks, usually

The use of veneer as a decoration, as seen on this fine William and Mary High Chest, became popular in the early eighteenth century.

ornamented the lowboy's working surface. Early William and Mary dressing tables typically featured six legs, four in front and two at the rear, with turned, inverted ball-cupped feet. Stretchers between legs might be straight, curved or x-formed. Later versions were more likely to have four legs and no stretcher.

A companion piece to the lowboy was the high chest, popularly called a highboy in later times. The high chest took the place of the Jacobean press and court cupboard. With a height of six feet in some instances, it consisted of a chest on a chest. Upper drawers were so high that they were best suited to storage of seldom-used heirloom linens and coverlets. Lower drawers, which were more accessible, might contain personal possessions. As with the first dressing tables, the earliest high chests often stood on six legs, with trumpet and cup turnings, ball feet,

and stretchers. Similarly, later high chests featured five or four legs and dispensed with stretchers. Pediments on chests of this period were invariably flat, with perhaps a simple overhanging molded cornice.

Given the imposing scale of the William and Mary high chest, it is not surprising that clients often were willing to spend more freely here for extravagant effects in terms of materials and workmanship. Particularly desirable were high chests whose surfaces were decorated with Oriental lacquerwork. A certain amount of this sort of exotica could be imported via the British East India Company, and some pieces made their way to American via smugglers, but for the most part Americans were satisfied to buy their fancy pieces from self-taught native cabinetmakers.

The sources of design motifs for these pieces were various – Oriental porcelains, calicoes and silks, Delftware, or even a rare imported chinoiserie cabinet if the cabinetmaker was lucky enough to know someone who owned such a prize. But for the most part craftsmen looked for inspiration to pattern books. The most influential volume was *A Treatise on Japanning*, written in 1688 by the English designers John Stalker and George Parker. Not only did the book include a panoply of Oriental images, albeit rather fantastic ones, but it also included some practical advice on such matters as creating raised designs with chalk compounds and preparing and applying the finest lacquer. On the subject of fixing metal leaf to wood, the writers counseled, 'Lay on your gold rightly, and if your work be sufficiently moist, you'll perceive how lovingly the gold will embrace it, hugging, and clinging it.'

Tables, by their utilitarian nature, seldom provided craftsmen with the opportunity for elaborate surface decoration, but they too became more specialized in purpose. Side tables, mixing tables, candlestands, and tables used specifically for dining, all become distinctive forms with proportions and features of their own. One form that has been identified as particularly American was the 'tuck-away'. Small, easily moved, and well-suited to use in rooms that were short on free space, the tuck-away featured a single gate and a top that folded flat

Left: The design of the high chest remained popular in less sophisticated New England towns during the first half of the eighteenth century.

against a wall when the gate swung closed. A variation which is considered equally American is the butterfly table. The name probably is derived from the butterfly-wing shape of the brackets that support the folding top sections. Splay-leg tables, their four legs angled outward for extra firmness, also seem to be a distinctive American table design.

England's Queen Anne ascended the British throne in 1702 and died twelve years later in 1714, but as in the case of the previous period, the decorative influences that bore her name were not clearly apparent in the Colonies for some time after her death. The basic conservatism of Americans and the slowness with which foreign examples became known to them, conspired to delay the flowering of the Queen Anne style until roughly 1725.

In broad terms, the new period was characterized by a refinement of those elements that had first appeared in the previous quarter-century. Room interiors whose furnishings had been an assemblage of individual elements, each one designed according to its own rules, became visually integrated. Furniture, windows, architectural moldings, panelled walls, related to one another in scale and decorative motifs. In furniture, the formal, straight lines, the reliance on turnings for decoration, so typical of the William and Mary style, were replaced with a repertoire of curved lines of more subtle, graceful character. In particular, the *cyma* or continuous double curve, pronounced 'the line of beauty' by English artist William Hogarth some years later, came to dominate the forms of everything from chair legs to the scroll tops found on high chests. The construction of pieces was also played down visually, so that no matter how complex the relationship of parts, they were hidden within curves. Carving, when incorporated in the design, was most often a variation on the scallop shell.

It was during this period that regional characteristics having to do with both design and construction evolved sufficiently to make it possible to distinguish furniture made in Boston or Newport from that made in New York or Philadelphia. Furniture historians generally agree on the following broad generalizations: Massachusetts furniture of this period tended to be conservative, with certain features of the William and Mary era lasting longer here than anywhere else. Individual pieces are typically

more slender, more vertical in proportions, than pieces produced in the other colonies. Newport, Rhode Island, which was becoming a furniture-making center of great activity owing to its prime position as an international port, favored crested silhouettes on the backs of its chairs and exotic woods and lead the way in introducing such detailing as the ball-and-claw foot and the blockfront, features usually associated with the Chippendale era elsewhere. New York, which still felt the influence of its original Dutch settlers, produced somewhat heavier, squatter, more sturdy furniture. And Philadelphia, fast becoming the most sophisticated center for furniture-making in the Colonies, was the source of the most refined, most skillfully ornamented, most nearly English furniture of all.

In terms of woods used, cabinetmakers everywhere continued to favor native black walnut and maple, but in places like Newport and Philadelphia, imported mahogany appeared with increasing frequency. Mahogany was, of course, an exotic wood, being a product of the West Indies. Evidently, its potential as a material for fine furniture had been slow to be

Left: *Japanning and chinoserie on a maple and pine high chest.* Above: *on a low chest.*

noted on either side of the Atlantic, for it is told that the first shipments of mahogany were brought into England not as lumber but a source of a medicinal substance believed to be similar in health-giving properties to chinchona (quinine).

Attitudes changed sometime after 1720 when a British ship captain brought back a sizable load of lumber as ballast and tried to persuade his house builder to use the stuff in construction. The carpenter reportedly refused on the grounds that 'Jamaica wood', as it was called, was simply unworkable, that the tools to cut and carve it did not exist. The captain persevered, however, and when he finally found a craftsman willing to try making a modest candle-box, he was amply rewarded for his efforts, Reportedly, the reputation of mahogany quickly spread and within five years it was competitive with walnut as a fine wood among English furniture makers. By 1735 the value of mahogany shipped to England annually had swelled to £6430 and by 1750 to nearly £30,000. In America mahogany became an infrequent alternative to walnut beginning around 1740, though there had been isolated instances of its use as early as 1708.

There was ample reason for mahogany's growing popularity. The wood was remarkably strong and resistant to warping and to worms. Uniform in its graining, it could be carved in the most intricate patterns. (The pierced work that became one of the most esteemed features of the Chippendale period could not have been possible in other woods.) Because mahogany was cut from virgin stands of huge trees, the boards obtainable were often exceedingly wide, making them ideal materials for the tops of tables and the fronts of large cabinets and chests. Mahogany also came in a range of beautifully rich reddish-browns and showed a superb affinity for polishes and lacquers.

While most of the types of furniture in vogue during this period had been introduced in the first decades of the century, virtually all of them showed certain modifications that represented improvements in comfort and utility. Nothing in furniture demonstrates the full measure of Queen Anne styling better than traditional side chairs of the period. Here we see virtually the entire vocabulary of the Queen Anne style brought together in a simplified, harmonious statement. The single most conspicuous element of this construction was the cabriole

Arm chairs might have upholstered seats, rather than cushions. The front cabriole legs have pan feet.

leg. The term cabriole, which was not actually applied to the Queen Anne leg until the Victorian era, derives from an Italian word meaning 'goat's leap' and, indeed, the supporting member does recall the profile of that lithe creature's hind leg. Wonderfully graceful in appearance, it also created a remarkably stable support system; the legs, in angling outward from the seat, rested on a wider base than was possible with straight legged chairs. The added stability reduced the furniture-makers' reliance on underframing, and stretchers began to diminish in importance. They disappeared altogether in some later versions of the Queen Anne chair.

So, too, the new 'bended back' of chairs represented an advance over the banister back of the previous era. Now, a single, broad, vase-shaped splat filled the space between chair back uprights. The splat's flatish surface was curved just enough to conform to the human spine. For the first time a sitter could actually lean back and get both support and comfort from a straight chair. The splat also provided a worthy surface for ornamentation: veneers of richly figured woods were occasionally applied to dress up simpler wooden chairs.

Queen Anne chair feet were also different from their predecessors. In place of the bulbous turnings of old were understated, carved leg endings. The plainest, known as 'Dutch', 'club', or 'pad' feet, were outward-swelling, rounded shapes. Slightly more elaborate were the slipper, webbed, and 'trifid' (meaning three-toed) designs, the last carved with ridges in a way that barely suggested an animal's foot. (This will develop into a true claw foot in the decades to come.) The only other carving was likely to be a shell motif, or secondarily a sun-burst or acanthus leaf, which was displayed

sometimes as the central ornament at the top of the chair back or seat rail, or on the foremost part of the cabriole legs.

During this period, upholstery came into ever-widening use. Easy chairs, a novelty in the previous period, became more common, and even straight chairs, such as were used at the dining table, were more likely to be cushioned and covered with cloth. To judge from contem-porary inventories, much of the finest fabric was imported from England and France, but a

Below left: The high chest, later known as a high-boy, was the eighteenth century equivalent of the press cupboard.
Below: Later in the century, high chests included architectural features like a broken pediment in their decoration.

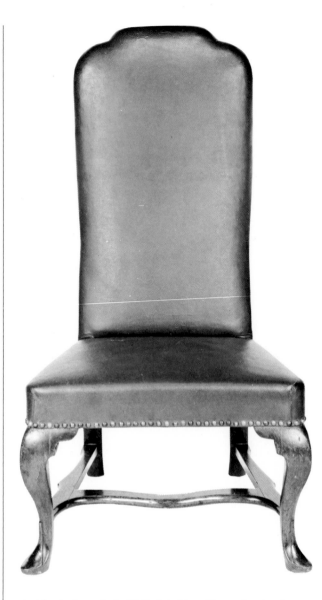

A side chair made in Philadelphia relies on its simple lines for decoration.

sive bedsteads with a substantial frame whose posts might reach as high as eight feet in some instances. The beadsteads were said to be of the 'camp' or 'tent' variety, meaning that they were outfitted with a tester, a tall framework for holding bed curtains and canopy. Sometimes the top of the frame was flat and sometimes it was arched, the latter a pretty solution to fitting a bed under the sloping eaves of an upper-story bedroom.

Desks, meanwhile, showed relatively little change, being chiefly of the slant-top variety. They are usually distinguishable from earlier models on the basis of their legs, decorative hardware and pigeonhole detailing. Legs typically were formed in the classic 'cyma' curve. Handle hardware, still imported, combined batwing mounts with simple bail handles. Pigeonholes evolved from simple open compartments to elaborate storage systems that combined open slots with drawers, closed ports and sometimes a dozen or more cunningly fashioned 'secret compartments'. The last might be accessible only if the right combination of hidden spring locks were pressed.

We have said that the Queen Anne period did not produce many new forms, but there are some notable exceptions among tables. For example, tea tables came into currency in conjunction with the growing popularity for tea drinking. The typical tea table was small, slender in proportion, with a narrow galley or molding surrounding the top. The top might be round or it might be rectangular; in some instances it was equipped with a 'birdcage' mechanism on the underside that allowed it to revolve or tilt up for storage. Because it was generally small in size, a pedestal base with tripod feet often provided the supporting structure.

Card or gaming tables also appeared at this time. The distinctive feature of the card table was the design of its top. Made in two equal parts, it hinged so that one folded over the other when not in use. In actual practice, the upper segment might be leaned up against a wall as a kind of decorative backsplash when the table top was not being used for card-playing. When the table was in play, it had to be moved away from the wall, a gate-leg swung out, and the freeswinging top extended. Because games were usually an evening amusement, the tables frequently had four rounded, enlarged corners

goodly share of the embroidery work was of local industry, produced by able wives and daughters for their own households. Crewelwork, which involved stitching decorative designs on a linen background, was particularly favored as an upholstery material during this period. Turkey work, the coarser form of needlework done in imitation of woven Turkish carpeting, was also used, though generally not in the most stylish households.

More comfortable chairs were paralleled by advances in bedding. In the more fashionable households, beds ceased to be simple lowslung frames for holding the mattress off the floor and became, in many instances, impres-

The tilt-top of a Chippendale pie crust table allowed for easy storage when not in use.

that were meant to hold candlesticks. One or more dish-like depressions in the surface were sometimes provided to hold dice or other game pieces, and a single drawer kept packs of cards.

Looking glasses, which was the contemporary term for any framed, mirrored surface that hung on a wall, had been exceedingly rare up to this time, but now the well-to-do might fancy such an addition to their best rooms. In most instances the glass was imported, the techniques for making large-sized reflecting glasses still being beyond the means of most Colonial artisans. But custom frames, small sized mirrors, and a certain amount of repair work on imported glass were available, as witness the advertisements appearing in *The New-York Weekly Journal* in 1735 under the name of Gerardus Duyckinck: 'Looking Glasses new Silvered and the Frames plaine, Japan'd or Flowered'. (Duyckinck supplemented his income as a glazier and framer by doing portraits and teaching painting on glass, a popular art form of the day.) Interestingly, in the relatively uncommon instances that American-made looking glass was used to ornament large overmantels or long pier frames, several sections of glass might have to be joined to fill the frame. Given the still crude state of the craft, the seams were always very evident. The frames, on the other hand, could be as fine as any other pro-

duct of Colonial Queen Anne furniture-making, with a finely scrolled crest above and apron below. Applied gilt ornaments, carved shell motifs and elaborate fretwork might also be featured.

It should be noted that for the first time individuality in the workmanship of a few master cabinetmakers emerged. Among the names and works that have survived to instruct furniture historians are Job Townsend and John Goddard of Newport, Thomas Johnston of Boston, and William Savery of Philadelphia. Savery began his trade sometime around 1740 and died in 1787, working 'at the Sign of the Chair, a little below the Market, in Second Street.'

The era of American Chippendale has been compared to the Golden Age in Greece and the High Renaissance in Italy, times when artists were no longer inventing a new style but perfecting its expression. And so it is that American Chippendale furniture, and the Georgian architecture that evolved with it, are generally regarded as the climactic phases of decorative artistic movements that began at the turn of the century.

An armchair with trifid feet designed by William Savery of Philadelphia.

The furniture style takes its name, of course, from Thomas Chippendale (active 1748-1779), who operated a thriving 'Cabinet and Upholstery Warehouse' at 60 St Martin's Lane, in London. Chippendale's far-flung fame derived not so much from his masterful skills as a cabinetmaker and carver, which were considerable, as from a volume of his designs published in 1754, entitled *The Gentleman and Cabinet-maker's Director*. The book, containing 160 engraved plates, was intended as both a catalog of his own works and a copy-book for others, including artisans of more modest attainments. 'Upon the whole,' the author writes, 'I have here given no Design but what may be executed with Advantage by the Hands of a skilful Workman, though some of the Profession have been diligent enough to represent them ... as so many specious Drawings, impossible to be worked off by any Mechanic whatsoever. I will not scruple to attribute this to Malice.'

Chippendale began his text with a short lesson in aesthetics. 'Of all the Arts which are either improved or ornamented by Architecture,' the author states, 'that of CABINET—MAKING is not only the most useful and ornamental, but capable of receiving great Assistance from it as any whatever. I have therefore prefixed to the following Designs a Short Explanation of the Five Orders. Without an Acquaintance with this Science, and some Knowledge of the Rules of Perspective, the Cabinet-Maker cannot make the Designs of his Work intelligible, nor shew, in a little Compass, the whole Conduct and Effect of the piece. These, therefore, ought to be carefully studied by every one who would excel in this Branch, since they are the very Soul and Basis of his Art.'

Good to his word, Chippendale used the first eight plates to show in detail the Tuscan, Doric, Ionic, Corinthian, and Composite orders. He then went on to display a varied collection of furniture designs and ornamentations that cabinetmakers could reproduce exactly or amend according to clients' wishes. 'Every Design in the book can be improved, both as to Beauty and Enrichment, in the Execution,' he assured readers with due modesty. Among the categories of furniture shown were 'Buroes, Breakfast-Tables, Dressing and China-Tables, Chairs, Settees, Sopha's, Beds, Presses and Cloaths-Chests, Candle-Stands, and Clock-Cases.' They were, he said, drawn variously from the 'Gothic, Chinese and Modern Taste';

the last-named might better be described as a simplified version of courtly French rococo.

The first edition of *The Director* reached American shores within a year of publication, and by 1776 there are known to have been at least 29 copies of the book in Philadelphia alone. Other English cabinetmakers followed Chippendale's example and issued pattern books of their own, which also found their way to furniture-making centers in the Colonies, but none ever became as influential as the first. Though the transition from the gentle, understated forms of American Queen Anne to the more elaborate, intricate scrolls and curlicues of American Chippendale, could be said to have had its roots before *The Director* came off the presses, Thomas Chippendale will always be remembered as the genius who gave the age its direction.

At the same time, Colonial interiors were changing, reflecting parallel developments in English manor house architecture. As with Chippendale, pattern books were the chief source of information for clients and carpenters on this side of the Atlantic. Batty Langley's *City and Country Builder's and Workman's Treasury of Designs*, published in London in 1739, was perhaps the best known of a half dozen or more builders' handbooks. Langley and his professional peers were, in turn, avowed disciples of Andrea Palladio, the great Italian classicist who had so persuasively interpreted the architectural principles of Ancient Greece and Rome.

The American Georgian, or Neo-Palladian, houses that were built in homage to these models tended to be somewhat less flamboyant, inside and out, than their English cousins. Interior decorations, which provided the backdrop for Chippendale-style furniture, were concentrated on fireplace walls, around important doorways and windows. Features such as broken pediment moldings, fluted pilasters, classic entablatures and cornices, frequently found their echoes in the elaborately carved bonnets of high chests and tall case clocks, in the pedestal bases of tea tables, and in the detailing of bedsteads. Though many hands might be involved in producing a finished, furnished interior, the overall effect was one of remarkable harmony, as though a single genius had orchestrated the entire compostion.

Right: A Chippendale bedstead is identified by the pencil-post headposts and ball-and-claw feet.

A George II tilt-top table with a needlework top might double as a firescreen.

More restrained, more conservative, too, were the furniture designs that issued from American workshops. Though there is the same lightness and refinement found in English examples, Colonial examples show less of the Chinese, Gothic and Rococo detailing than their Old World counterparts. Carving, which in Chippendale's own work was delicate to the point of dangerous fragility, was more substantial in American pieces. The cabriole leg, which all but disappeared in England, to be replaced by the square-sectioned straight leg, remained popular in high-style American furniture until after the American Revolution. Likewise, the ball-and-claw foot, which was featured in English furniture beginning around 1730, and which Chippendale had long since discarded before he published the *Director*, became prominent in American furniture design only after 1750. Mahogany became the preferred wood, especially for pieces in which precision carving was featured, but virtually all master cabinetmakers continued to work in native walnut, maple and cherry, as well. And among furniture forms, many Queen Anne types persisted with little change other than ornamentation – the desk-and-bookcase, the high chest, the slope-front desk, card tables and tea tables, easy chairs and lowboys, to list the most prominent.

For all these holdovers, however, American Chippendale introduced a number of distinctly new features to the American scene. As always, the place to begin such a survey is in chair design, most especially in the design of side chairs which, by their nature, were the purest expression of Chippendale artistry. The feature which most clearly gave witness to the style was the chair back.

At the height of the Queen Anne period, it will be recalled, the top and side rails joined together in a *cyma* curve that was intended to look all but seamless. The one-piece vertical backspat was relatively simple, with the extent of its decoration being limited to gentle urn-shaped curves along the margins. Maturely-formed Chippendale chairs, by contrast, discarded the continuous back rail in favor of outward-flaring, almost straight, side rails and a separate horizontal 'yoke' or top rail. The yoke might take a 'cupid's bow' shape, with the ends curving upward almost like handgrips; or, less frequently, it might round downward at the corners to meet the side rails.

Back splats were variously solid with the urn-shape elaborated into a succession of large and small curves; or pierced. In pierced work, which required the skills of the finest carvers working in the most uniformly-grained mahogany, the

A square tea or card table with 'Chinese' fretwork, in the style of the Goddard-Townsend workshop Newport, RI.

In the eighteenth century, arm chairs were usually found in bedrooms, for the use of invalids.

artist strove to create lacy patterns of wood while serving the basic requirements of chair stability and back support. Pierced slats were executed in a great variety of designs. The majority, which were vertical, took their inspiration from rococo cartouches; Gothic trefoils, quatrefoil, and lancets; interlaced scrolls and ribbands; and Chinese lattice and fretwork, the last-named freely adapted from Chinese porcelain and wallpaper patterns. Less commonly, the back-splat function was handled horizontally, with a succession of pierced splats running ladder-fashion in parallel curves between the side rails.

The chair legs of American Chippendale, as we have said, might be either cabriole or straight, the latter in emulation of Thomas Chippendale's so-called 'Marlborough' style. (In discussing chair legs, it is well to remember that we are talking about front legs only; the rear legs of virtually all chairs were left plain, inasmuch as they were usually tucked against a wall out of sight.) Cabriole legs might be elab-

orately carved, especially over the knees, or unadorned. In either instance, they typically ended in a 'claw-and-ball' foot. This latter device seems to have been ancestrally Chinese and was said to represent the three claws of the revered Yellow Dragon, grasping a pearl. The claw-and-ball apparently came to Holland by way of Dutch East India Company trade goods in the late seventeenth century. From there it crossed the English Channel in Queen Anne's time, coming into widespread use in England around 1730. The claw-and-ball foot appeared

Made in two sections, the chest-on-chest was based on the high chest but provided more storage room.

Individual cabinetmakers would adapt and modify Chippendale's basic plans to create a distinct chair design.

occasionally in the Colonies beginning around 1735 but became fashionable only around 1750 when the transition from Queen Anne to Chippendale began. In the finest-carved examples, the claws appear almost lifelike in their grasp; the ball, which is the actual support point of the chair leg, was sometimes nearly round, but more often it was flattened on the underside for greater stability. Straight legs might be surface-carved with Gothic tracery, fluted, or plain. They typically ended without ornamental feet of any kind.

The finest American Chippendale chairs were produced in Philadelphia, which was by the 1760s the second largest and most prosperous English-speaking city in the world.

Among the hundred or more registered furniture-makers at work there, the following names are outstanding as makers of superior Philadelphia Chippendale chairs: Benjamin Randolph, Benjamin Gostelowe, William Savery, Thomas Tufft, James Gillingham, Thomas Affleck, John Elliott Sr, John Folwell, Jonathan Shoemaker, Daniel Trotter, and Ephriam Haines. (These same masters also are identified with some of the finest cabinets, tables, desks, and upholstered pieces.)

American Chippendale chairs represent the apex of high-style furniture-making in the Colonies in the period between 1750 and the Revolution, but high-style is only part of the story. The windsor chair, one of the most graceful and utilitarian American furniture forms ever created, came on the scene about this time too. In terms of sheer numbers, it can be called the pre-eminent chair of the Chippendale generation, though in virtually every particular, this popular piece diverges from its soignée cousin in design.

The ancestors of the windsor chair were apparently first produced by itinerant English craftsmen living in and around the beech forests of Windsor, a forested borough some 20 miles west of London. The craftsmen, who were skilled turners rather than joiners, made their chairs the only way they knew how – from an assortment of vertical and horizontal spindles or 'turned-all-over' sticks. A plank seat, pre-drilled with sockets, held the variously sized legs, arms and back spindles and these, in turn, were braced on to another with top rails and stretchers. Admirably easy and inexpensive to construct, variations on windsor-made chairs apparently became commonplace in country households throughout the region.

The story is told that King George I 'discovered' the design while out hunting in the woods about Windsor Castle. Seeking refuge in a peasant cottage during a rainstorm, he was given a stick chair in which to take his ease. He is said to have been so impressed by the comfort and simplicity of the chair that he ordered his cabinetmaker to reproduce the design. Whatever the truth of the story, history records that early in the eighteenth century the gentry began buying up windsor-style chairs for the garden, the terrace and the kitchen. London

The hooped back of the Windsor chair was made from a single piece of a pliable wood, such as hickory or ash.

One of the popular variations of the Windsor chair was the settee.

The comb-back Windsor armchair was popular around Philadelphia.

chairmakers evidently tried to dress up the genre by replacing the center spindles with a carved, pierced splat but the effect remained somewhat clumsy-looking. Inasmuch as joiners' and cabinetmakers' chairs were becoming *de rigeur* among the fashionable, these native designs rarely were chosen for formal English interiors.

When the chair's descendants reached the Colonies, however, their reception was quite different. Fine joiners and cabinet-makers being relatively few in the early decades, turners and carpenters of more modest abilities found a ready market for their wares among people of every station. The first center of American windsor-chair making was Philadelphia, where examples may have been turned out as early as 1725. But it was not until mid-century that craftsmen of that city can be said to have developed a distinctive American-style windsor. Though the chair eventually was produced up and down the Atlantic Seaboard, it was widely known as the 'Philadelphia chair'

There are six basic windsor types, named according to the style of the back. The first ones

made in Philadelphia were low-backs (horseshoe-shaped backs); they were followed by comb-backs, bow-backs (also known as hoop-backs and sack-backs), and New England armchairs (featuring a continuous hoop-and-arm design). There were also writing-arm windsors, equipped with small, flat surfaces on one side; windsors with a drawer under the seat and/or the arm for keeping needlework, reading or writing material; and windsor highchairs, cradles, and settees.

The American windsor was typically lighter and more graceful in appearance than the English version, yet its construction afforded it superior strength and durability. This admirable combination was made possible by the American custom of using not just one wood throughout, but a variety of woods, each one selected according to its particular properties of resilience, strength and so on. Hickory and ash, which were tough and springy, and could be counted on to yield to the pressure of the occupant's back, were chosen for the hoops and spindles. (The finest chairs might have as many as eleven slender spindles.) A single piece of knot-free pine was easily drilled with a row of sockets (for the legs, arms, and spindles), and carved into a saddle-shaped seat. And maple, chestnut, birch or ash, close-grained and strong, were lathe-turned to make stick legs and stretchers. The chair was assembled when the woods were still green. As they cured, the chair became stronger, the various woods tightening up on each other. Neither screws or nails were ever used, though wooden wedges were sometimes driven through the tops of the legs to secure them more tightly in their sockets. A coat of paint, most commonly dark green or apple green in the early years, a rainbow of colors later, was applied to hide the joiners' construction tricks.

The chairs became so popular in America after the 1750s that there were furniture-makers in virtually every city that found it profitable to specialize in their manufacture. By the Revolution, it would seem scarcely a household or tavern was without some windsors, and their popularity continued undiminished into the next century. Carpenter's Hall, Philadelphia, where the signers of the Declaration of Independence gathered in 1776, was evidently

This library bookcase or china cabinet is copied almost exactly from Chippendale's Director.

The writing armchair was the forerunner of the school chair frequently found in lecture halls.

furnished with a score or more windsors. George Washington bought 27 of them, at a price of $1.78 each, for his portico at Mount Vernon in 1796. And just five years later, Thomas Jefferson purchased 48 black and gold windsors, at an inflated price of $4 each, for Monticello.

Coincident with the growth of the American windsor chair, the rocking chair first appeared during the American Chippendale period. Its invention was once credited to Benjamin Franklin, who is said to have attached iron bends to the legs of an ordinary chair around 1760; why people would think this eminently sensible notion had not been tried earlier in Europe is something of a puzzlement, inasmuch as rocking cradles had been around from at least the Middle Ages. The first rockers were either ladder-back, rush-bottomed country chairs or American windsors. Their legs were equipped with curved runners, called 'carpet cutters', almost as an afterthought. The conversion was accomplished in one of two ways: either the tips of the legs were whittled down for insertion into sockets in the runners or, if thick enough to permit it, the legs were slotted at the bottom and the runners inserted in the

The bombé or kettle base was still popular in the Boston area well into the late eighteenth century.

Nonetheless, they seem to have enjoyed wide acceptance as furnishing for the bedroom, the nursery and the kitchen.

The chairs made between 1750 and 1789 demonstrate native skill and inventiveness in small compass, but a survey of the Chippendale period reveals that virtually every sort of furniture reached new heights of perfection and decorative opulence. High chests and chests-on-chest, for example, were never grander than in these years. Nathanial Hawthorne, describing the genre later, spoke in awe of 'chests which stand on four slender legs, and send an absolute tower of mahogany to the ceiling, the whole terminating in a fantastically carved ornament.' Made in two sections, they stood seven feet high or more and carried massive bonnets and incorporated an elaborate display of flame- and urn-shaped finials, elaborate relief carvings and classic fluting and reeding. Drawer hardware was usually pierced or solid 'willow' mount with bail handle. The finest high chests came from Philadelphia and were made in the workshops of Thomas Affleck, William Savery and Benjamin Randolph. Many high chests were made with companion low boys or dressing tables.

Secretaries, which combined a desk with storage space for books above, were also more imposing and tended to be crowned with a massive cornice. These too were likely to be made in two sections to facilitate moving, and they might even have brass handles on the sides for carrying. Built on the same scale but usually less opulent were linen presses, which were the American equivalent of the French armoire. These featured an upper story cabinet in which to keep clothes on hangers, resting on a separate three-drawered chest.

The chest of drawers, which is a term usually used to denote the single story three- or four-drawer chest, remained an extremely popular and necessary item of furniture in the Chippendale era. But its overall form was often modified by a certain amount of Baroque shaping. Massachusetts cabinetmakers, including Benjamin Frothingham, John Cogswell and George Bright, became known for using the *bombé* or kettle-base, which featured a front and sides which swelled outward. The Townsend-Goddard family of Newport, Rhode Island, made a speciality of the block-front. This involved carving a recessed panel into the fronts of each of the drawers so that when they

slots and pins or dowels run through to hold them. Early rocking chairs, like rocking cribs, featured rather short rockers whose curves were the same fore and aft; as their popularity increased and experimentation continued, the rear portion of the runner was extended for greater stability. Rocking chairs evidently did not find their way into the formal rooms of households in the eighteenth century, owing to their homespun character, and they were never shown in the pattern books of cabinetmakers.

were all in position the recess presented a uniform plane. Other cabinetmakers in other centers fancied serpentine, oxbow, breakfront and still other shaping devices as a means of adding three-dimensionality to their work. (Shaping, of course, added considerably to the labor involved in producing a finished cabinet, and was more costly of materials, so one can assume that these pieces were comparatively more expensive than their Queen Anne predecessors.)

In the category of tables, the changes were less noticeable, with virtually all the forms that had proved themselves useful in the earlier part of the century continuing to be made. The one notable addition was the pembroke table, supposedly named for a lady client who wished to have a small, portable table on which she might breakfast in the bedroom. The pembroke featured a wide stationary top and narrow drop leaves, thereby reversing the proportions of the more conventional drop-leaf table.

The Chippendale Style remained popular into the 1790s, surviving the upheavals of the American Revolution and the political break with England. Curiously, neither the clients nor their cabinetmakers seem to have troubled themselves unduly over their continuing links with English artistic traditions and, when the

Above: *The stretchers of this Pembroke table reveal a Chinese influence.*
Below: *The Pembroke table usually had two drop-leaves and a small drawer.*

war was over the connections were forged anew, in the Federal Style which was America's version of English Neoclassicism.

3
The Federal Period

As a new United States of America emerged in the aftermath of the Revolution that brought it independence from Britain, a new style of furniture was also to take hold in the last quarter of the eighteenth century. The fledgling nation had proclaimed its political autonomy, but it remained heavily dependent on England in matters of culture and taste. During the 50 or so years from about 1780 to 1830, now generally known as the Federal Period, the new nation tried not merely to copy English fashion but it took what Europe had to offer and created furniture that was distinctly its own.

One of the less expected influences on this Federal style was the neoclassical movement in the arts, which began to gather momentum in the latter part of the eighteenth century in England as well as in America. It came from several sources. One was the discovery of the remains of Pompeii and Herculaneum in Italy earlier in the century. This sparked an interest in classical antiquity among cultivated people on both sides of the Atlantic. Then, too, the new republic of the United States found itself often looking back to republican Rome for models and motifs – so that Washington and his fellow founding fathers were portrayed in togas like Roman senators. And what could be more appropriate for the world's newest democracy than to adopt and adapt furniture styles from the world's oldest democracy?

American national pride, then, was at a peak, and citizens who preferred imported furniture over American-made were apt to be derided as 'Tories' (much the way autoworkers in the 1980s denounced people who bought Japanese cars). Imitating English furniture styles, however, was a different matter, and design books published by British cabinetmakers were an easy way to transmit the new neoclassical furniture fashions to the New World.

Architect Robert Adam was the leading proponent of the new style in Britain. A Scotsman by birth, he had traveled in 1754 to Italy and Dalmatia, where he studied the classical ruins firsthand. Adam was critical of early classicists like William Kent and Andrea Palladio, whom he felt were overly influenced by such heavy classical architectural elements as pediments and columns. Adam focused on

Previous page: Neoclassical elements of design can be seen in both the furniture and the architecture of the large dining room at Mount Vernon.

Roman interiors like Diocletian's palace at Spalato. In collaboration with his brother, he published the influential *Works in Architecture of Robert and James Adam, Esquires* in 1773, showing airy and light reinterpretations of the neoclassical style which emphasized function. A furniture-designer as well as an architect, Adam demanded utter harmony between his architecture and furniture designs.

Only the very rich might have the means to acquire Adam's furniture, but London cabinetmakers quickly copied his work and popularized it for the general public. Two in particular have become synonymous with English furniture of the period, George Hepplewhite and Thomas Sheraton. Neither of these cabinetmakers was thought of as particularly important in his time, but their

The shield-back side chair was one of the most popular Hepplewhite designs.

claimed Hepplewhite's designs were old-fashioned. Thought by some to be more original than Hepplewhite, Sheraton had served as a journeyman cabinetmaker but saw himself first and foremost as a draftsman. In contrast to the delicate inlaid and carved furniture of essentially linear form by Hepplewhite, Sheraton was known for his use of turned or reeded supports with bowed or hollowed facades and his more fiercely rectilinear forms, tight in profile. Sheraton's chairs tended to be square-backed, with tapering reeded legs and projecting elements.

While distinctions can be made between these two London cabinetmakers, in the final analysis the two very often overlapped in style and both owed their ideas to Robert Adam. Still another English cabinetmaker whose work was copied on the other side of the Atlantic was Thomas Shearer, who published *The Cabinet-Maker's London Book of Prices, and Designs of*

The secretary bookcase designed by John Aiken for George Washington has a tambour closing.

The square back design of a Sheraton chair includes small-scale details.

copies of the new neoclassical styles set the fashion for American furniture at the beginning of the Federal Period. Hepplewhite's book, *The Cabinetmaker and Upholsterer's Guide*, came out first, in 1788. An obscure London craftsman, Hepplewhite made no particular claims for originality. His book was brought out by his wife after his death. Hepplewhite's interpretations of the new neoclassical furniture showed curvilinear features and carved ornament. His chairs had straight, tapering legs square in section, with flaring, bracket or spade feet. The backs were shield-, heart- or oval-shaped.

Thomas Sheraton, whose design book, *The Cabinet-Maker and Upholsterer's Drawing-Book*, was published in four parts from 1791 to 1794,

The front drawing room at Boscobel incorporates many neoclassical details.

Cabinetwork in 1788. Such London design books listed the rate of pay for all basic furniture forms shown, as well as costs for optional details. In this way, they offered American cabinetmakers basic furniture forms in the current style with plenty of room for individual variation.

Perhaps the earliest piece of furniture in the new Federal style was a portable writing desk, made in 1775-1776 by Benjamin Randolph for Thomas Jefferson. The two men were friends, and Jefferson stayed with Randolph in Philadelphia while he attended the first and second meetings of the Continental Congress. A simple piece, the desk sits on the lap and distinguishes itself as Federal Period with a band of string inlay. Jefferson has written that he used the desk to draft the Declaration of Independence.

When Washington built the banquet hall at Mount Vernon in the period from 1776 to 1785, he bought 24 Sheraton-style chairs from Philadelphia cabinetmaker John Aiken to furnish it. Reflecting the typically American preference for simplicity over a more Continental ornateness, Washington said of the plans for the banquet hall, 'it is my intention to do it in a plain, neat style; which, independently of its being the present taste (as I am informed) is my choice.' In 1797 Washington purchased a handsome tambour secretary and bookcase of mahogany, white pine and yellow poplar from John Aiken for $145.

An immediate effect of the Revolution was to bring on an economic depression, but it didn't take the nation long to recover and enter a new era of prosperity and concentration on commercial activity and trade. Life in America, however, was still predominantly rural and agrarian. At the time of the Constitutional Convention, there were fewer than four million people in America. Of those who were employed, 90 percent were farmers, and the country had no paved roads until 1800.

The population grew by leaps and bounds, fed in part by great waves of immigration. If importing furniture was frowned upon, immigrants nevertheless brought their own furniture with them – as well as their cabinet-making skills, in many instances. Often trained in the furniture centers of England or Europe, immigrant cabinetmakers not only brought the latest fashions with them, but spurred American craftsmen to keep up with the new styles or lose out in the competition for customers. Despite American chauvinism, many prominent citizens did import furniture.

Mrs William Bingham, who ruled society in Philadelphia when it served as the nation's capital, was one of English furniture merchant George Seddon's American customers, and her lyre-back drawing room chairs came from Seddon's London furniture shop. John Quincy Adams, Benjamin Franklin, George Washington, James Madison and James Monroe are all known to have imported or bought French furniture in the neoclassical style. Thomas Jefferson brought 86 crates of furniture back with him from Paris where he served as Minister to France from 1784-1789. Later, stiff tariffs discouraged the practice of importing. In fact, in 1807 Jefferson himself was responsible for a Trade Embargo Act which checked the import flow of both furniture and hardware used in cabinetmaking.

Furniture made outside major centers used simpler details and native wood. The ogee bracket feet are typical of the Georgia Piedmont.

Fostered by the influx of trained cabinet-makers from abroad and the encouragement the Federal Government gave to home industry, the American furniture business grew. In the largest metropolitan areas, work was quite specialized. In addition to cabinetmakers and chairmakers, the biggest shops might also support inlay artisans, carvers, gilders, upholsterers and other specialized workers. The new neoclassical Federal style created a demand for inlay makers who could supply stringing, banding, pictorial and figured inlay, as well as veneer by the yard. While it might seem otherwise, inlay work is not a particularly reliable method of identifying the place of origin of Federal furniture because it could be, and often was, supplied by artisans from near and far. When tariffs didn't make the cost prohibitive or embargoes prevent their use, metal hardware, brass and enamel fittings, ormolu and exotic woods were some of the items often imported.

The creation of the new American union encouraged solidarity and organization among furniture-makers. As the states ratified the Constitution one by one during 1787 and 1788, many American cities held parades to celebrate. In New York, the makers of windsor chairs marched under a banner praising free trade and the new Federal Union and proclaiming 'O'er all the world our chairs are found.' Price-fixing and wage-fixing were probably common practices in Philadelphia.

Houses of the Federal Period tended to have large windows and spacious rooms, which were especially suitable for showing off to best advantage the small-scale, delicate detail of Federal furniture. The new prosperity of Federal America meant greater affluence, larger houses, more entertaining and more furniture. In addition to the greater simplicity which characterized American furniture, American efficiency and pragmatism found expression in the development of new forms of furniture. Especially popular were secretary-desks, work tables, basin stands, night tables, sideboards with enclosed cupboards and drawers, cellarettes, knifeboxes and pianoforte cases.

One of the most imposing pieces of furniture in a Federal home was the secretary, which consisted of a desk with an enclosed bookcase on top. A cultured Federal family might have books of history, philosophy, religion, geography, astronomy, classical mythology, agriculture and botany, which were kept in the upper portion of the secretary. Letter-writing was an important task in those days because it provided the only method of long-distance communication. Copies of letters were usually made since it often took many months before a reply came and the correspondent might forget the contents of the original letter. So the secretary, or breakfront as it is more commonly called in the twentieth century, became the repository for correspondence and family records. It was probably the single most costly piece of furniture a family might own.

The design of desks and secretaries changed dramatically in the Federal Period. Slant-top desks and bookcases in the Chippendale style continued to be popular and might be updated with neoclassical carving and inlay as well as a swan's neck pediment. Federal desks, however, usually had a secretary drawer which pulled out with a drawer front that folded down to form the writing surface. The drawer was often flanked by Roman or Greek columns.

Less common were cylinder-fall desks, with a curved lid that dropped back into a case. The appearance of the lady's desk indicates the new emphasis on women educating themselves. The tambour desk, or lady's writing table, had shutter doors made of narrow strips of wood glued to canvas. Another variation of the secretary was the heavy, squarish, fall-front version based on the French *secrétaire à abattant*. By 1815, *The New York Book of Prices* showed 28 different patterns for the muntins (wooden strips between glass panes) on secretaries. Secretaries were not confined to the drawing room or parlor, but might also appear in a bedroom.

A New England contribution to new furniture forms in the Federal Period was the tall-backed, upholstered chair with open arms, called a Martha Washington or 'lolling' chair. No one is sure how this chair got to be named the Martha Washington, but the term 'lolling' chair appears on eighteenth-century and early nineteenth-century bills of sale and inventories. Connoting a physical attitude of grace and ease perhaps appropriate to the style if not to American industriousness, this chair was attacked in *Gentleman's Magazine* as a 'two-armed machine adapted to the indulgent purposes of lolling.' Very few lolling chairs have any carved ornament, as befits the plain style of Boston and most New England furniture. One

The tall back and slim tapering arms identify this as a 'lolling chair'.

such chair, however, stamped with the name S Bedlam, does have daisies, pendant husks or bellflowers above stop fluting.

The most common easy chair style was the standard, wing-backed wing chair patterned after a Hepplewhite design. It was not unusual to outfit such chairs with chamber pots under a loose cushion when they were used in a bedroom. The horizontally rolled arms of the eighteenth century easy chair remained popular into the 1820s. What gave this furniture form a Federal Period look was the lightening of the wings and arms, along with tapered or turned legs. Other fashionable upholstered chairs were inspired by French styles. The bergère has a lower, round back than the wing chair, while the fauteuil was normally made with a low, square back.

The late eighteenth century brought a revolution in seat design. The heavy, solid construction of Queen Anne and Chippendale chairs gave way to light, delicate, even fragile chairs which were easy to move around. Changes in ornamentation followed changes in construction with veneers, inlay, low relief and small-scale carving becoming popular. The fact that so many and such a variety of chairs from the Federal Period have survived is one indication of their considerable popularity.

Windsor chairs were used in every room of the house by the Federal Period. Older forms like the sack-back and the low-back chair con-

Inlaid shells can be seen on either side of the drawer of this Hepplewhite card or side table.

tinued to be made, but other styles also became popular. Bow-backed and oval-backed windsor chairs made an appearance in the 1780s. Bow-back windsor chairs usually had a cushion. The fan-backed form was preferred in New England. In the 1780s it was often braced by two spindles, ending in a block pinned to the back of the seat. During the Federal Period, in place of bolder vase and ring-shaped turnings, windsor chairs had simpler turnings which imitated bamboo. They were made in a variety of colors by the 1790s: white, yellow and black being the most common. In 1795 the New York chairmaker Walter MacBride advertised windsor chairs 'Japanned any colour and neatly flowered.' In 1796 George Washington ordered two dozen from Gilbert and Robert Gaw of Philadelphia and paid $44 for them all.

By 1800, square, rod-back windsor chairs were popular, and in the 1820s, the ball-back style took precedence. In terms of construction, all of these various styles of windsor chair were related to Sheraton 'fancy' chairs, the name given to painted furniture. The parts could be made and shipped all over the country as 'knocked down' or 'shaken' chairs. Such chairs were also exported, in particular to South America and the Caribbean. In 1791 alone, 4000

Card tables with elaborate inlay and carving were frequently made and sold in pairs.

windsor chairs were shipped to the French West Indies, 533 to the Dutch West Indies, 144 to the Danish West Indies and 24 to Africa.

Other popular chair styles were the Boston and Salem rockers. The Salem rocker was developed after 1810. It had bamboo turnings,

flat, shallow-scooped seats and a painted tablet for the top rail. The Boston rocker emerged in the 1820s and had spool turnings, a seat which rolled up in back and scrolled shoulders on its tablet. Low-backed captain's chairs continued to be used during the Federal Period. The less expensive version of fancy chairs had rush seats and stenciled decoration instead of upholstery, carving and brass mounts. Such furniture eventually became known as Hitchcock chairs. (Lambert Hitchcock, whose furniture was to become famous later in the nineteenth century, first began making chairs in Barkhamsted, Connecticut, in 1818.)

As household rooms became more specialized, so did other forms of furniture. Particularly as French styles grew fashionable, gilded or painted furniture became popular at the turn of the eighteenth century. Not just chairs, but all painted or gilded furniture went by the name of 'fancy' furniture. One of the more idiosyncratic furniture forms in use was the lady's work table. Designed for sewing and needle-work, these tables usually had a silk bag attached like a cocoon to the underside of the table. Its purpose was to hold fancywork. Sometimes the silk bags were gathered or pleated; other times they were draped flush with the table legs like a woman's skirt and trimmed.

A Boston contribution to the new variety of furniture forms was a table made to fit between

of which swung on internal metal rods to provide greater stability.

Three types of mirrors are especially associated with the Federal Period. A looking glass called a horse or cheval consisted of a tall mirror suspended between two pillars and hung by means of two center screws. It was also at times called a screen dressing glass. Mantel mirrors of the Federal Period came in three sec-

Above: *The elaborate carving on a New York sofa is accented by stencils.*
Left: *The lyre was a popular neoclassical symbol frequently used in furniture.*
Far left: *Fantastic animal forms were also used on some federal furniture.*

the architraves of windows and called a pier table. Another specialized form which gained currency in the Federal Period was called a Mixing Table. Designed for mixing drinks, one appeared on an 1809 White House inventory, listed by Thomas Jefferson as 'an elegant mahogany drink table with a marble top.' Card tables were frequently made in pairs during the Federal Period in order to maintain the symmetry of furniture arrangements. While they were designed for playing loo or whist and might have a backgammon or chess board inlay, their primary function was ornamental. The 'mechanical' card table had three legs, two

tions and during the later portion of the era featured heavy, turned balusters. Carved cornucopias and foliage often decorated the frame.

Another mirror style popular from 1805 into the 1850s was circular with a convex mirror, which gave a fish-eye reflection. Called a girandole, it was usually gilded and decorated with an eagle with spread wings and dolphins. The bald eagle had been chosen by the Continental Congress as the national emblem in 1782. While Benjamin Franklin claimed to prefer the turkey on the ground that it was 'a bird of courage and would not hesitate to attack a grenadier of the British Guard,' eagles were generally very popular, and appeared everywhere as a patriotic symbol. Another popular decorative emblem was George Washington's portrait, which served as a symbol of constitutional liberty. Still another frequently used symbol was the Freemasons' all-seeing eye of God set against a pyramid, which still appears on the back of the dollar bill.

Before 1820, only the houses of the rich were apt to have sofas, couches and settees, but greater affluence and changes in lifestyles made this type of furniture fashionable and widespread in the later part of the Federal Period. Sofas appeared most often in drawing rooms or parlors, but might also be found in bedrooms and halls. The square-back Sheraton style sofa was particularly popular. It had upholstered arms and turned, detached arm supports which extended to the floor to form the legs. The sides and back of such a sofa might be caned and the panels above the crest rail were usually carved or veneered. The sofa was often placed near the fireplace, with a firescreen nearby and perhaps a sofa table with short drop leaves would be put in front of it, the equivalent of what today is called a coffee table.

Three sofa styles were the most popular toward the end of the Federal Period. The plain style was also the cheapest and was based on the design of the Roman couch. It had a long, wooden crest rail and fulcra with scrolled ends. Reeding, carving and veneer added to the sofa's elegance and it might have lion's paw feet. The most striking versions incorporated Roman-style dolphins. The Grecian couch, also called a double scroll sofa, was illustrated in the 1828 *Philadelphia Book of Prices*. These sofas were often made in pairs to flank a fireplace. When they were designed for reclining, they might have one end of the back higher and then would be called a Récamier, after the painter David's portrait of Mme Récamier, or else they were termed meridiènnes. Grecian couches were also sometimes called 'napping' couches. The square back sofa was the third style. The cabriole sofa was a variation that eliminated the square look of the upright back posts by employing continuous upholstery.

Some sofa tables had reeded sabre legs in the Sheraton style, but by 1820 heavy, curved or carved pedestal legs with lion's paw feet were the fashion. Others rested on four scrolled supports called standards, or sometimes on dolphins, caryatids or lyres. Marble tops were not unusual. The gueridon was a smaller version of the center or sofa table and was inspired

The Federal architectural tenets emphasizing high ceilings and large windows seen in the Brinckerhoff dining room. (State Museum of Pennsylvania)

Dining room tables could expand to seat extra guests by using leaves.

by Grecian models. One version with three monopedia was copied from a table discovered in a garden in Herculaneum. Gilded brass or ormolu added richness and was imported from France until the Trade Embargo Act cut off the supply. From then on, furniture-makers relied increasingly on stenciling and gilding.

Rooms used exclusively for dining were found in American houses at the end of the eighteenth century. Federal Period dining rooms did not have a large table placed in the center of the room as is the style today. Instead, dining tables were made in two or three parts with leaves so that they could be moved easily and they were placed against the wall or even in a hallway. The massive, gateleg tables of earlier eras were banished from the stylish Federal home. Dining tables and other furniture acquired a new mobility in the Federal Period through the use of casters or rollers. Such devices had been concealed on Chippendale furniture, but by 1800, they were a visible and integral part of the design. Other appointments of the Federal dining room included the dumbwaiter, a drum-shaped table with a revolving frame of three shelves which could be used for wine glasses or tea cups. Few dumb waiters have survived, probably because they were used too much to be easily preserved. The urn stand was a piece of furniture designed to support the classical Sheffield hot water or tea

urn; it might have an inset marble top.

Probably the most important innovation in American furniture of the Federal Period could be found in the dining room. It was the sideboard. Unlike the simple side table of colonial times, a Federal sideboard might have an elaborate combination of cupboards, drawers and cellarette compartments. It has been said to have evolved from Robert Adam's practice of putting urn stands or knife boxes at either end of a serving table.

The sideboard gradually grew in size over the years becoming more massive and eventually resting on short turned or carved legs. While English sideboards incorporated a metal-lined compartment for keeping wine cool, the American taste was for separate wine coolers, which were put under the sideboard. Such wine coolers were called cellarettes. Usually they were lined with lead or copper, banded with brass and frequently had lion-mask ring pulls. The sideboard had simplicity of form but not construction. Advances in technology made possible the great size and sweeping shape of the sideboard, and the development of layers or sandwiches of wood glued together had permitted a new freedom in form and ornament. Hepplewhite's design book declared that sideboards were 'so well received that a well appointed dining room was incomplete without one.'

Above and left: The accordion action table before extension, and extended without leaves. This particular table is said to have belonged to President Martin Van Buren.

Related to the sideboard but more typically southern, like the cellarette, was the huntboard. These tall tables of shallow depth evolved to serve large groups during the festivities which followed the hunt. They were usually placed in the hall or on the porch, where it was more convenient to serve men and women freshly returned from riding and apt to be covered with mud from the fields.

Federal bedrooms of the affluent usually featured a high post bedstead with posts that reached to a height of seven feet or more. The posts might be carved or otherwise decorated, as they were on the imposing bedstead made for Elizabeth Derby of Salem circa 1808. The cornice of that bed, which was gilded by John Doggett of Boston, has been attributed to William Lemon of Salem. Such beds would be richly appointed with drapes and valances, as well as spreads. Matching bedhangings, upholstery and curtains, however, were probably only enjoyed by the rich.

More modest households might have what was called a field bedstead. Its five and a half foot posts were more suitable to a lower ceilinged house. According to Sheraton's design book, field bedsteads 'receive this name on account of their being similar in size and shape to those really used in camps.' The preferred dressing for such a bed would be white curtains of the batiste-like sheer cotton called mull, or dimity, the striped white cotton which was like modern-day seersucker. Other more modest Federal beds included the low post bedstead with four foot posts. This type of bed was not designed to carry a canopy frame. The simplest beds were known as 'cott' bedsteads. Today they would most likely be called attic beds since they were frequently kept there and used by servants or to accommodate an overflow of guests.

None of these beds would have conventional box springs; the mattresses would be supported by ropes which were tightly laced across the frame. In any household the bed was a piece of furniture with a high value. By the time horsehair mattress and down-filled ticking were put on the frame, such beds put the user quite high off the floor. When that was the case, bed steps or library steps would be provided to help the very young, the old or the infirm to climb into bed. Some such steps were designed to conceal a chamber pot or 'night convenience.'

A new type of bed became popular around 1815. It was called the French or sleigh bed, and one by Charles Lannuier of New York had wheels attached to metal braces to enable easy rolling. Gilded eagle heads adorned the head of this type of bed. A form of canopy known as a balduchin might be attached to the wall over the head of such a bed, which usually had foot and headboards of the same height.

In the Federal Period, houses were still being made without closets, with the exception of shallow ones with hooks for hanging coats or nightclothes. People continued to use chests, wardrobes and clothes presses. Often made with full-length doors, wardrobes had sliding trays, shelves and sometimes space for hanging dressing gowns and coats.

The bathroom as we know it today did not exist in the Federal household, so that a common piece of furniture found in the bedroom was the basin or wash stand. Square or circular in shape, or else made to fit into the corner of a room, the basin or wash stand was made with a basin hole and cup holes for items like soap and toothbrushes. Each was equipped with a basin and pitcher for washing. English cream ware and stone ware were popular, but so was Chinese porcelain. The wash stand usually was placed near a window for proper lighting and had high splash boards along the back to protect the walls from water. Many were made with a center leg in front to prevent tipping. While the basin sat in the opening provided for it on top of the wash stand, the pitcher was kept on an open lower shelf or in the cupboard below.

Another piece of furniture which might appear in the Federal bedroom or dressing room were the dressing tables. They were usually square-topped descendants of the eighteenth-century lowboy. Sometimes they were called Beau Brummells after the British dandy George Bryan Brummell, who died in 1840. Some had small handkerchief drawers and a swinging mirror, a form which quickly became typical for all dressing bureaus of the period and eventually for all dressers in the nineteenth century.

The dresser or bureau took a distinctive form in the Federal Period, sometimes having a deep top drawer which could be used to store large items like blankets or quilts. Such a feature was known as a tablet drawer since it often mimicked in design a tablet and cornice; it became the focal point of the entire piece of furniture. In other cases, the Federal bureau had a tablet drawer and two or three smaller drawers above. While in England the designation 'bureau' meant a square-topped desk, by 1792 in America it quite definitely meant a four-drawer chest. The typical bureau had flaring French feet, a scrolled skirt and a straight, bowed or serpentine front.

Probably because of widespread familiarity with the design books from England, regional furniture during the Federal Period became more subtle. If any one city was the focus of fashion in furniture at the end of the eighteenth century, it was Philadelphia. Home of the first American banks, it retained shipping supremacy until 1797. George Washington lived there from 1790 to 1797 during his two terms as President, while the new city, Washington, was under construction and the City of Brotherly Love served as capital. In the period from 1790 to 1810, the population of Philadelphia, which painter Gilbert Stuart had celebrated in neoclassical spirit as 'the Athens of America,' was said to have doubled from nearly

This dining room sideboard looks simple in design but the joinery and veneer mark it as the work of a master craftsman.

Above: *A cellarette by Charles-Honore Lannuier rests on sphinxes painted 'antique vert', which simulates the patina of ancient bronze.*

50,000 to almost 100,000. The city reestablished the export trade, which the Revolution had stopped, and sold goods to both Britain and France. Furniture reflected the greater conservatism of old Philadelphia families, in contrast to newer cities like Baltimore, which had rather fewer moneyed families before the Revolution.

The great Philadelphia cabinetmakers of the Chippendale Period had died or retired by the last decade of the eighteenth century. In their place came a generation, including Daniel Trotter, who made popular mahogany ladder-back chairs which had carved and pierced slats, as well as the typical Philadelphia rounded shoulders. John Aiken's chairs had heart or fan backs, while Henry Connelly and Ephraim Haines both made squareback chairs, Connelly's with three-quarter turned colonettes and rounded spade feet. Haines was a Philadelphia Quaker who apprenticed to Daniel Trotter in 1791. After he married Trotter's daughter, Haines inherited his business in 1800. Reflecting a growing trend, Haines

Mrs Dyckman's bedroom at Boscobel contains a Federal secretary and a comfortable wing chair. An adjustable pole screen stands near the fireplace.

was a cabinetmaker-entrepreneur, as much business manager as craftsman. When Haines received an order from Stephen Girard for a set of black ebony furniture, he put seven craftsmen to work. Rather than make the pieces himself, Haines chose the designs, supervised the work and warranted it.

John Davey, who worked in Philadelphia from 1797 to 1822, produced a Sheraton-style secretary distinguished by its strong oval patterns in sharply contrasted woods, with relatively low relief carving. Thomas Affleck made a set of armchairs in 1791-1793 for the House of Representatives and the Senate while the Capitol was still in Philadelphia. The chairs

reflected the basic form of the French armchair, but were simple and lighter in form and design as befitted the new style.

The work cycle of a furniture-maker during this era was still much as it had been for centuries. It began with an apprenticeship at the age of 14 or 16 to a cabinetmaker, working six days a week. At 21 the apprentice master became a journeyman, doing piecework or working for wages. Once he accumulated enough money, the now-experienced artisan would usually go into business for himself, either alone or in partnership with another journeyman.

The rapid increase in population in Phila-

delphia caused growing pains in the furniture business there. As furniture shops expanded beyond the small shops where customers had played a significant role in the design process, frictions developed. Commission furniture warehouses might retail pieces by a number of different cabinetmakers so that customers bought finished products now, although custom-made furniture could still be 'bespoke' or put on order. As warehouses grew in popularity, cabinetmakers did less and less commission work. Stockpiling and speculation became common, and it was increasingly necessary to standardize the most popular items. When a cabinetmaker sold to a retail outlet, it wasn't easy to pass on increases in his labor costs to the customer. The result was that cabinetmakers began to rely more on apprentices, shutting journeymen out of the market.

Discontent among journeymen led them to organize, and in 1794-1795, the Philadelphia journeymen published their own price list, *The Journeyman's Cabinet- and Chair-makers Philadelphia Book of Prices*. The Federal Society of Philadelphia Journeymen Cabinetmakers was not looked upon favorably by the master cabinetmakers, and the conflict escalated. Members of the Journeymen's Society refused to work in the shop of a master who would not pay fixed wages. They opened their own warehouse and sold directly to the public, in an attempt to bypass their former bosses. The conflict went on for two years until 1796, when the journeymen won their demands for a six-day, eleven-hour-a-day work week and wages of one dollar a day. When *The Cabinetmakers Philadelphia and London Book of Prices* was issued in 1797, it contained what may be the earliest example of an escalator clause in a trade union agreement. The agreement read, 'whenever the necessaries of life, house-rent, etc., shall rise above what they are at present, the Employers agree to advance the per centum to what shall be agreed on.'

Business continued to expand and diversify. In addition to warehouses, mail ordering was introduced. Increasingly, only the wealthiest could afford 'bespoke' furniture, so furniture-makers produced what was called 'shop work.' The economy was shifting from barter to money, but cabinetmakers still bartered, sometimes taking in old furniture in trade. If a craftsmen couldn't afford to operate his own shop, he would have his work auctioned for a

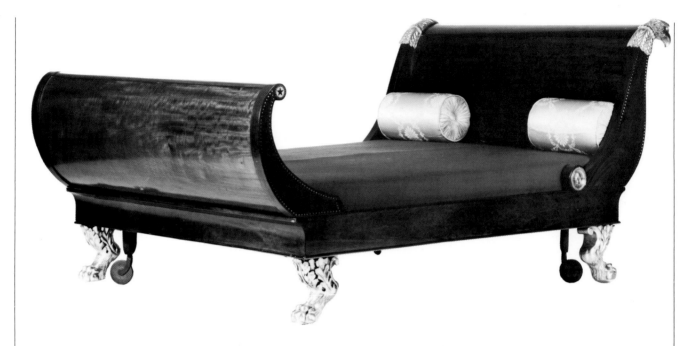

The sleigh bed, like this one designed by Lannuier, was a departure from the fourposter popular since medieval times.

fee of 10 to 12½ percent. (One such auction business, T B Freeman & Son, which was started in 1805, now bills itself as Samuel T Freeman, the oldest auction house in America.)

Philadelphia was a magnet for French emigrés, particularly in the Federal Period after the French Revolution, with the result that Federal furniture made in Philadelphia shows a strong French influence. Included among the emigrés were John James Audubon, Alexandre Le Sueur and Pierre Charles L'Enfant. With them came a vogue for gilded and painted Louis XVI furniture which was further stimulated by the importation of French furnishings after the collapse of the *ancien regime*. Plans were even made for a special, never-to-materialize retreat on the Susquehanna River for Louis XVI and Marie Antoinette, and the visiting Duke d'Orleans proposed marriage to the socialite daughter of William Bingham. Bingham is reputed to have told the Duke, 'Should you ever be restored to your hereditary position you will be too great a match for her; if not she is too great a match for you.' Some 10,000 to 25,000 French immigrants ended up in the Philadelphia environs after the French Revolution in 1789, and many of them were cabinetmakers.

While Philadelphia furniture of the period 1800 to 1810 can sometimes be identified by its French-influenced gentle and undulating carving, Boston carving was quite sharp. Phila-delphia had passed Boston in population mid-way through the eighteenth century, and one explanation for the more conservative furniture which Boston produced has been that Boston attracted fewer immigrants in the early nine-teenth century.

Newport, which had been an important New England cabinetmaking center earlier, lost 40 percent of its population during the Revolution, with the result that cabinetmaking there declined. Both the destruction of the war and the laws against Newport's slave trade led cabinetmakers to set up shop elsewhere. Boston, the hub of New England, also suffered, falling to third in population in 1790, behind Philadelphia and New York. Those cities had drawn off much of Boston's business when the British blockaded the port. Boston bounced back, though, and along with nearby Salem produced some of the finest American Federal furniture.

One Massachusetts family in particular took an interest in cabinetmaking of the period and commissioned a number of the finest Federal pieces from New England. Elias Hasket Derby was a Salem seafarer who, like other enter-prising nautical Americans, turned to priva-teering during the Revolution. Derby established markets for America in Spain, France, the West Indies and the East in the period after the Revoltuion. A sofa made for the

Derby family in 1800 reflected the fashion of the day in its mahogany border ornamented with rosettes and glyphs, its sweeping back and its scrolled arms. The style probably came from Hepplewhite's design book.

Derby had the distinction of becoming one of New England's first millionaires, and he built a house in Salem to match his new affluence. He commissioned two of Boston's best cabinet-makers, John Seymour and his son Thomas, to make much of the furniture for his new house. A wine cooler the Seymours made for Derby has tapered, carved and fluted legs and dramatic vertical bands of alternating light and dark wood. Not long after Derby's house, designed by architect and jack of all trades Samuel McIntire, was finished in 1799, both he and his wife died. The house, described by a visitor as 'more like a palace than the dwelling of an American merchant,' was demolished and its furnishings scattered in 1815, the result of a squabble among the heirs.

Derby's daughter Elizabeth, who had married the sea captain Nathaniel West and then divorced him, taking back her maiden name, continued her parents' interest in fine furniture. She commissioned Thomas Seymour to make a particularly handsome mahogany commode in 1809, and the bill for the piece came to $80, plus another $10 for the seashells painted on the top by John Ritto Penniman, a Boston artist. The commode, which has been called 'one of the supreme achievements of American cabinetmaking,' incorporates the four basic methods of ornamenting furniture: carving, veneering, inlaying and painting. The shells painted by Penniman in the lunette on top of the commode are so clearly rendered that they each can be identified: panther cowrie, moon shell, murex, common wentletrap or scalaria, Bursa rana and harp shell.

A chest-on-chest made for Elizabeth Derby in 1796 has been attributed to William Lemon. Made of mahogany and pine, it was probably

The Greco-Roman revival of the early nineteenth century made adaptations of ancient styles popular in various guises.

A serpentine-front chest of drawers from Wilkes County, Georgia, is made of native black walnut and yellow pine.

carved by Samuel McIntire. Like so many craftsmen of the day, McIntire had more than one skill. In addition to serving as the architect for Elias Hasket Derby's Salem house and doing the carving on much fine furniture in the Boston area, he worked as a carpenter, a designer, a sculptor and a musician. One of the few crafts he apparently did not involve himself in was cabinetmaking, but snowflake punchwork background carvings from Salem are usually attributed to him. Bills he sent to Salem cabinetmaker Jacob Sanderson in 1802 and 1803 show that he did carving for the top rails of that cabinetmaker's sofas. He also did carving for another Salem cabinetmaker, Nehemiah Adams, making the pieces more than simple copies from Sheraton's design through his carving.

The Seymour father and son who made furniture for the Derby family had emigrated from England to Portland, Maine in 1784 and then moved to Boston in 1794. A five-chairback settee from their Boston shop shows the increasing emphasis in sharp silhouettes and sabre-shaped legs in the classical Greek style that characterizes Federal furniture. Another piece made by the Seymours was a movable gaming table called an Occasional. One of the most distinctive pieces of furniture by the Seymours is a pedimented tambour desk with a fold-out writing surface. It is not a design which appears in the English design books and may have been inspired by the Louis XVI furniture form called a *bonheur-du-jour*. Owned by Eliza and Benjamin Proctor, the desk has extremely fine inlay, patterned in such a way as to create a sense of movement. The narrow stringing creates a contrast of light and dark lines.

Such inlay was made by drawing the designs on paper and then pricking through the original to make copies. A copy was then pasted onto a thin slice of wood. Many different woods might be used: satinwood, holly, rosewood, snake, zebra, boxwood, yew, maple, birch. Layers of wood would be clamped in a vise and the design cut with a saw. An entire design might be laid out and glued together until the cabinetmaker bought it. Shading was achieved by putting the wood in hot sand to brown.

The style of secretary and bookcase with an inlaid pediment-on-pediment patterned after a Hepplewhite design was made frequently enough in the Boston area to be called the 'Salem' desk. It was used for writing, keeping accounts and holding the family or individual's library. A number are ornamented with carved pomegranates or with a beetle crawling out of a shell. A similar inlay pattern appears on looking glasses and card tables, indicating that there was probably an inlay specialist in the area producing it.

The health of the cabinetmaking business in the Boston area is demonstrated by the fact that by 1835, there were 275 cabinet- and chair-makers working in Boston. Others had shops in nearby Newburyport, Ipswich and Marble-

A square chest of drawers believed to have been made by Thomas Seymour uses contrasting wood for decoration.

head. The most successful craftsmen formed the Massachusetts Charitable Mechanics Association in 1795. Some years later, the organization held exhibitions to encourage good craftsmanship.

Another cabinetmaker who worked in Boston from 1808 to 1815 was Samuel Gragg. Unlike such Boston artisans as William Appleton and William Hook, Gragg was essentially a country craftsman who came from rural New Hampshire. Gragg patented in 1808 the technique he used in his Elastic Chair, which is the first piece of American furniture to use bentwood as a basic structural element. Adopting the Grecian klismos form, Gragg used single strips of wood he had bent through heat and moisture – 75 years before what is now called bentwood furniture arrived on the scene – to make the back, seat and legs in a single, continuous sweep from the stile and side seat rail through the front leg. Gragg's side chair was illustrated in Thomas Hope's 1807 *Household Furniture and Interior Decoration*. Some of the chairs, which usually were painted, were decorated with peacock feather designs.

If Philadelphia set the furniture fashions during the first half of the Federal Period, it was New York that did so during the second half. Washington's inauguration was held there in 1789 at Federal Hall, which had been built in

A Hepplewhite desk has tambour slides covering the pigeonholes.

anticipation of New York becoming the nation's capital. The furniture in Federal Hall was designed in the Louis XVI neoclassical style by Pierre L'Enfant. L'Enfant is said to have introduced reeded legs to American furniture. The city of New York itself was experiencing a rapid economic growth at the end of the eighteenth century. In 1804 alone, 700 new buildings went up, and between 1800 and 1810, the city's population increased by 36,000 to a total of a little below a million, 94,400, the largest of any city in America.

As the nation moved into the nineteenth century, furniture-makers moved away from the delicate interpretations of neoclassicism towards heavier, more archaeologically accurate interpretations of the classical past. America's first fully trained architect, Benjamin Henry Latrobe, was probably the most influential designer to promote the Greco-Roman revival of the late Federal Period. Latrobe, whose wife was a childhood friend of Dolley Madison's, called himself 'a bigoted Greek.'

Latrobe drew his inspiration from Thomas Hope's 1807 book, *Household Furniture and Interior Decoration*. In turn, Hope had been influenced by Charles Percier and Pierre Fontaine, who were to become Napoleon's official court decorators. Percier and Fontaine made scale drawings of ancient Egyptian and Roman furniture on which designs the official style of the French Empire were based. Latrobe was commissioned in 1809 by President Madison and his wife Dolley to design furniture for the Oval Room of the White House. Baltimore cabinetmakers John and Hugh Findlay executed Latrobe's design. Such forms as the Greek klismos chair, with sabre legs, and the Roman curule chair, with legs in an X pattern, were the order of the day. In general, furniture became more solid, more heavily sculpted and deeply carved, relying on a mix of French influences and English Regency style.

The War of 1812, called by some the Second War for Independence, put the United States directly at odds with England again, and when the British burned the White House, Latrobe's furniture was lost, but not the new styles he introduced. The end of the war brought a resurgence of American nationalism. Scenes of US naval victories, for example, were a popular subject for drawings painted on mirrors through the 1820s. The British blockade during the war shifted the commercial emphasis from shipping to domestic manufacturing.

New York was at the center of the changes in fashion. The city had been made a dumping ground for surplus British products which had accumulated during the naval blockade. The tremendous growth in trade helped to make it the center of American cabinetmaking in the nineteenth century for a number of reasons. In addition to having become the nation's biggest city, New York was a major port, but had easy access to the interior domestic markets on the Hudson River. These would be extended by the construction of the Erie Canal. New York merchants also served as the middlemen for the South. The city had 100 cabinetmakers and craftsmen by 1805.

Using new technology, Samuel Gragg bent the oak back and seat slats of this white oak and maple chair.

No single cabinetmaker's name is more synonymous with the Federal Period than that of Duncan Phyfe. Born in Scotland, he emigrated to Albany with his family at the age of 15. In 1792, the New York Directory listed him as a joiner. By 1794, he appeared there as a cabinetmaker. More an entrepreneur than an innovator, Phyfe ran a highly successful business. Good fortune had brought him the business of the powerful New York merchant John Jacob Astor. At his shop on Fulton Street, Phyfe was reputed to have employed the largest number of workmen under one roof of any establishment up until 1825. He kept several dozen journeymen and apprentices busy filling orders and was known by reputation as far away as Alexandria, Virginia.

Phyfe is recognized as a popularizer of Sheraton and Regency style furniture rather than as a totally original designer, although his best work has a distinctive feel. Typical of his work were acanthus carvings simplified into

A bookcase desk modeled after patterns set out in Sheraton's Cabinet Directory *incorporates glass painting in its decor.*

formalized patterns of ridges and grooves. Phyfe's furniture also employed reeding – reeds tied with ribbons and swags of drapery tied with tassels. The set of furniture that Phyfe made for Louisa Throop in 1808 is typical of his best in the late Federal style; it consisted of a Grecian couch, a console table with ormolu mounts, a *secrétaire à abattant* with Doric columns, a lyre-back chair – a Phyfe trademark – and a French bed with brass mounts in the Egyptian style. The Egyptian style and motifs that were apt to appear in furniture of this period were an offshoot of the Greco-Roman romantic classical trend. These Egyptian elements were transmitted to America primarily through the French Empire-style furnituremakers, who in turn had been affected by the discoveries and published drawings of ancient Egyptian works that came out of Napoleon's Egyptian expedition. Blatant Egyptian motifs and lines were never to become much more than an exotic sideshow for the

main productions of American furnituremakers of this period.

When Phyfe died in 1854, his estate was valued at half a million dollars, a most impressive sum for that day and proof of an industrious and thrifty craftsman. Ironically, fewer than 20 different pieces of furniture survive with Phyfe's label or some other accepted form of documentation. Many pieces that once were sold and bought as 'by Duncan Phyfe' are now regarded as simply being of his period and style.

Another influential New York cabinetmaker of the age was French-born Charles-Honoré

Right: *A mahogany chest-on-chest has an allegorical pediment carved by John or Simeon Skillin of Boston, who usually made ships' figureheads.*

Lannuier. Lannuier was one of the few New York cabinetmakers who actually had European training, and work was strongly influenced by French Directoire and Empire styles of furniture. He worked for the most distinguished New York families and was especially known for his stunning tables. In 1819, for instance, Lannuier finished a type of table known as a gueridon with an inlaid marble top and legs capped with bronze female heads. This is now in the Red Room of the White House.

Still another leading New York cabinetmaker was Michael Allison, who had a shop on Vesey Street, not far from Duncan Phyfe's. A card table by Allison has a vase pedestal with incurved legs and a clover-leaf folding top and could easily be mistaken for Phyfe's handiwork. Allison's writing and sewing table has lyre supports. While these men were the best-known New York cabinetmakers, in fact many craftsmen, both native and immigrant, readily adapted to what was a New York style of furniture. The shield-back chair was a favorite New York pattern, and the yoke-back chair with rush seat and pad feet was popular to the north in the Hudson Valley. New York style ornamentation included shield-shaped key-note escutcheons and quarter-fan inlays on doors. Wardrobes were particularly popular in New York, and the *New York Price Book* of 1810 listed a winged wardrobe with carved rosettes, drapery and thunderbolt motifs which was one of the most expensive pieces of furniture of its time. In contrast to New England, where alternating light and dark inlays were in vogue, New York furniture makers favored solid mahogany.

In the period from 1790 to 1810, Baltimore became a major seaport rivaling Philadelphia and New York. This was because of its position at the hub of the tobacco and grain trade of the upper Chesapeake Bay. As as result of its commercial success, it attracted cabinetmakers emigrating from England, who produced a distinctive furniture rich in decoration and inlay. Particularly characteristic of Baltimore craftsmanship is the brilliant fire or striping found in the veneer ovals of furniture. Another Baltimore style is the tassel motif inlay found running down the legs of chairs and sofas.

A cylinder-fall desk and bookcase thought to be made in the Baltimore area between 1800 and 1810 employs a subtle combination of curved and straight lines in a pattern of banded veneers. Baltimore served as a principal market for the South, and kept some 50 cabinetmakers and painters, including John and Hugh Findlay, busy making furniture. Painted 'fancy' furniture was particularly popular in Baltimore. Another fashion of this city was the use of painted glass or *verre eglomise*, depicting classical scenes or 'views adjacent to the city.' The hallmark of the Findlays, such painted glass was used in mirrors and clocks.

A monumental secretary bookcase has pleated silk curtains and simple stencilling.

Below: *A rose- and satinwood Lannuier card table uses a gilded caryatid as a support.*

Above: *The heavy feet and pillars decorating this sideboard and cellarette point to the Victorian style.*

Most southern cities acquired their furniture elsewhere, rather than developing their own industry, but there were exceptions. There were no major cities in the South aside from Charleston before the Revolution, so most of the earliest southern furniture dates from the Federal Period.

Inland from western Virginia through the Carolinas into Georgia was the Piedmont, a region with strong middle-class traditions. Distinctly southern furniture from this area includes the huntboard, the cellarette and the sugar 'safe.' Since sugar, like coffee, tea and spices, was a particularly valuable household commodity, Southerners stored it in locked chests which sometimes were kept in the sitting room. Furniture from the Piedmont area showed a Pennsylvania influence, since many settlers had come down the Great Wagon Road from Philadelphia. Many furnituremakers doubled as farmers. Jesse Needham worked from 1793 to 1839, producing a distinctive furniture style with triangular pediments. William Little, who came to North Carolina from England through Charleston, was one of the few Piedmont cabinetmakers who worked in mahogany. He is also known for his capped tear-drop inlay, as well as a four-petal flower inlay. One of the best known groups of craftsmen working in the Piedmont was the Swisegood school in the Yadkin Valley.

Charleston, South Carolina, had been settled in the late seventeenth century, and by the mid-eighteenth century it was a thriving metropolis, its affluence fed by the rice, indigo and cotton trade. While English culture dominated, it was a cosmopolitan city with French, Dutch, German, Irish, Scottish and West Indian settlers. The wealthy plantation owners got much of their fine furniture from England, but local

furniture from the Federal Period reflected the influence of New York, which eventually replaced England as the major source for furniture there. Cypress was plentiful in the region and often used as a secondary wood in Charleston-made furniture. Characteristic of Charleston furniture was the use of rice plants to ornament objects like bed posts. To provide for better air circulation during the hot southern summers, the heads of bedsteads made in the region could be removed.

In the Deep South, the wealth created by a cotton economy meant that furniture could be imported, so that local cabinetmaking traditions never really developed. The exception was in New Orleans, which with its French connections produced two great craftsmen, Prudent Mallard and Francois Seignoret, both of whom were born in France. One of the contributions

A pair of painted side chairs made in Baltimore still have their original resist-dyed cotton upholstery.

Above: *Phyfe used many of the classical styles, like the curule stool, in his furniture.*
Left: *The Phyfe Room at Winterthur contains several examples of that master cabinetmaker's work.*
Below: *An armoire made in Missouri shows French influence in its design.*

Furniture makers in the back country of Pennsylvania adapted the fashionable forms to suit themselves.

to Federal furniture made by New Orleans was the 'campeachy' chair. Named after the state of Campeche in Mexico, it has a hammock-like bottom and is one of the few furniture forms of the era to show a Hispanic influence. Despite its French heritage, Louisiana had been a Spanish colony from 1762 to 1803, when the French regained it and then sold it to the United States. Early in the nineteenth century, New Orleans became the distribution center for New York furniture, which was sent there to be trans-shipped all over the Mississippi River Valley. Perhaps influenced by this commerce, the native New Orleans furniture thrived. By 1822, there were 50 cabinetmakers, 4 carvers and gilders, 5 chairmakers and 22 upholsterers listed in the New Orleans City Directory.

No survey of Federal furniture would be complete without a discussion of the traditions of American country furniture of the period.

Left: *A southern-made kitchen chair has a foot-controlled flywhisk attached to the back and bottom rungs, which allowed the cook to work with both hands and keep flies away.*

While city furniture might set the trends, America was still primarily a rural nation and the bulk of its population were country people who didn't buy furniture from urban cabinet-makers. Country furniture represents the tastes of ordinary people rather than the wealthy. As a result it tends to be more conservative and tradition-bound. Specialized crafts like inlaying or carving could not alone support a craftsman working outside of an urban area. The cabinetmaker had to rely solely on his own talents. The benefit of that was a great individuality in workmanship. What the country craftsman lacked in training and sophistication, he made up for with bright, contrasting colors, emphatic ornament and strong silhouettes.

In some cases, country furniture reflects the particular ethnic make-up of the region's settlers. The Germans who emigrated to Pennsylvania, popularly referred to as Pennsylvania Dutch, brought with them the traditional massive Baroque furniture of their native land. The tulip was a favored ornamental motif, along with carnations, hearts, birds, stars and geo-

Above: *A parlor piano by Jos Hisky.*
Below: *The Karshner Parlor, Winterthur.*

Right: *The Empire Parlor at Winterthur shows many classical influences.*

Away from the center of commerce and design, cabinetmakers used paint rather than complicated veneers to decorate furniture and paneling. (The Catawba Dining Room, the Museum of Early Southern Decorative Arts)

metric designs in bold, brightly painted patterns. The piece of furniture most typical of this style was the painted dower chest. Incorporating designs related to manuscript illumination, the dower chest was usually made for a girl of eight or ten. It was often decorated with unicorns, the symbol of virginity, and it held handiwork, personal belongings, blankets and linens in anticipation of the girl's eventual marriage.

Other forms of country furniture distinguished through regional characteristics. In this case, the nearest urban style center, like New York, Philadelphia or Boston, wielded influence over what was produced. Connecticut reflected the influence of New York as well as of Massachusetts and Rhode Island. Many Connecticut cabinetmakers had emigrated from rural England, and it came to be said of their furniture, 'if it is different, it's from Connecticut.' Reflecting the state's English ties, the chest on chest had great popularity in Connecticut. Carving was more subdued than that from Philadelphia, but also more idiosyncratic. Geometrical fans, sunbursts and pinwheels were popular forms of carving.

A rural New Hampshire family, the Dunlaps, produced a distinctive form of furniture in that state. Beginning with a typical ball-and-claw foot, the Dunlaps turned it into their own. They modified the conventional New England fan ornament by broadening the lobes until they looked like spoon handles. Dunlap carving on cornices had a basket weave appearance, and their gadrooning, called 'flowered ogee,' appears on many pieces from the area.

Rural western Massachusetts developed a characteristic furniture through the work of Daniel Clay of Greenfield, then the center of the rich agricultrual area of the upper Connecticut River valley. Clay served as the windsor chairmaker for the area. He also made fancy chairs with bamboo turnings and later on produced Grecian style chairs. Like many rural craftsmen, Clay expanded into carriagemaking, but when that proved uneconomic, returned to producing furniture exclusively.

East Hampton, on Long Island, now a popular summer place for New Yorkers, was a country town during the Federal Period. The Dominys of East Hampton were a well-known family of cabinetmakers at the time. Much of their work was devoid of the characteristics of any one particular style, which was agreeable to their conservative customers.

Since country cabinetmakers relied more on barter than their urban counterparts, their furniture was more evenly distributed throughout the community. A bill owed a merchant might be paid off with a piece of furniture by the local cabinetmaker. A good indication of the country of origin of a piece of furniture was often the mix of woods used. The top and legs of a country table, for example, might be mahogany while the apron was made of pine.

The country furniture industry was necessitated by the difficulty of transporting goods crosscountry. Imported furniture didn't often make its way into the rural regions. Mahogany was too expensive to ship, so craftsmen used local woods like cherry, maple and walnut. Once the systems of transportation began to improve in the second quarter of the nineteenth century, the country cabinetmaker found himself unable to compete with city furniture, and he was forced out of business.

As the Federal Period drew to a close in the 1830s, the nation was moving rapidly towards industrialization. The telegraph and the railroad were on their way. Furniture became more massive and ornate, eventually leaving behind the heavy dependence on fashions from other countries and older civilizations.

The Germans who settled in Pennsylvania were known for their painted blanket or dower chests.

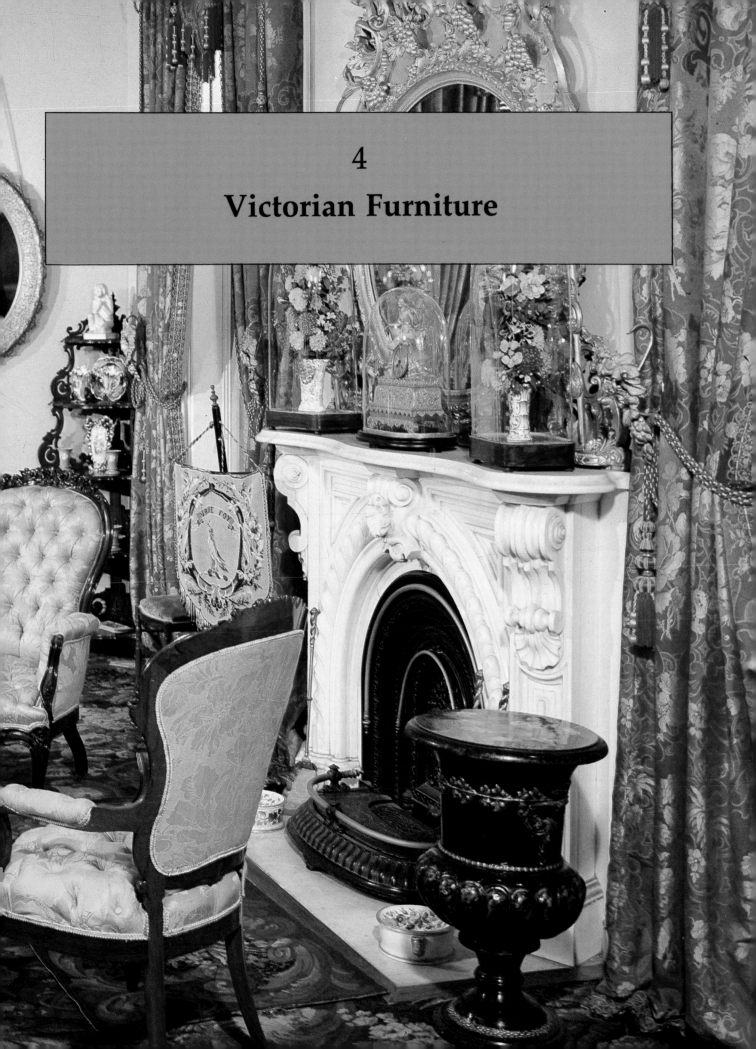

4
Victorian Furniture

As with the furniture of every age and every land, some context and perspective are necessary before examining – and criticizing – individual pieces and styles of the Victorian Age in America. For there can be no denying that many of the more stereotyped Victorian pieces of furniture have, until quite recently, been the object of some scorn, if not outright derision. But in the last couple of decades, two major changes have produced a new perspective on nineteenth century American furniture. One is a more catholic or tolerant aesthetic, a broadening of taste that now is willing to encompass a far more varied spectrum of styles in many fields, including furniture. The second

Previous page: *The Parlor of the Colonel Robert J Milligan House, now in the Brooklyn Museum, typifies the elaboration and exuberance of the Victorian era.*

Samuel Gragg's 'elastic chair,' patented in 1808, was the first American furniture to use bentwood as a structural element.

change has come about through a far broader and more detailed knowledge of the many different types of furniture produced throughout America during the nineteenth century. What was long regarded as 'Victorian furniture' was only one of many styles popular.

Beyond that, it is obvious that most of the familiar furniture from museums and paintings and photographs, and on which we base so many of our generalizations about Victorian America, are atypical set pieces. In many cases these were commissioned by those who maintained 'society' through such material trappings. Many of these pieces were custom designed and very expensive, beyond the reach (and probably the taste) of the growing urban and rural population. Much of this furniture conventionally regarded as Victorian was deliberately imitative of European models, while a far more indigenous and vernacular tradition of furniture making was actually being supported by many Americans.

For at the same time that such well publicized or 'High' style furniture-makers as Phyfe, Belter, Mallard, Meeks and others were providing furniture for the well-to-do and usually Eastern and urban families, Americans by the thousands were moving steadily westward, ripping out prairie sod to plant crops, cutting down countless trees, and building houses. They were establishing their existence while their cousins in the East were solidifying theirs, and their furniture would reflect this.

By about 1850, the region between the Great Lakes and the Ohio River was no longer considered frontier. Furniture factories were flourishing in such cities as Cincinnati, Ohio, and Grand Rapids, Michigan. They had access to raw materials and transportation, and could move goods relatively cheaply by either river or rail. By 1860, factories of all kinds in America were employing over a million people and the annual value of goods produced was close to $2,000,000,000 (worth far more in those days than such a sum now). The average worker earned about $1.40 for a 10-12 hour day – and would gain only about 60 cents by 1870, although by then the manufacturers' income had doubled.

There were several reasons why the country developed so rapidly during this period. One was the Civil War, which created a sudden demand for manufactured goods and so speeded the growth of factories. Another was

A neoclassical pier table decorated with gold leaf and stencils might be placed between two windows.

the Federal Government's protection of industry through loans, grants, and tariffs. In fact, the government had begun instituting tariffs back in 1816 to protect American industries, particularly from British competition. Meanwhile, the new railroads benefited both from the government's largesse and the new industrial needs: in 1831 there were only 73 miles of railroads in the United States, the line connecting Baltimore to Point of the Rock; by the 1860s there were more than 30,000 miles of railroad; the transcontinental railroad would be completed by 1869. This transportation system was vital to the development of American industry.

So much of what is taken for granted today was only developing during this era. Here was a country not one hundred years old and already perfecting the steam engine, sewing machine, telegraph and many other such advances to society. By the 1840s, Americans were traveling regularly across the Atlantic on the Cunard Steamship Line and picking up the latest in English and Continental fashions. In 1866 the transatlantic cable was laid, connecting America to Europe via the telegraph. Before the turn of the century, the typewriter, telephone and many other marvels would be invented. Small wonder that Americans of this era seemed to be full of themselves, their inven-

The gothic style is best exemplified by the chairs and matching table designed by the architect Alexander Jackson Davis for Lyndhurst.

tiveness and power. They were at once called 'the most grasping nation on the globe' by Alexis de Toqueville and praised for their ingenuity and energy.

All of this can be seen, and must be kept in mind, when considering the ways that Americans furnished their houses during the Victorian Age. The Empire style associated with Duncan Phyfe and Lannuier, for instance, would be carried into the early Victorian period, but it presaged some of the characteristics of the later decades by becoming heavier. While the design of much of the furniture of the 1830s retained the interest in the ancient Greeks, the execution of designs was not so delicate. Furnishings of all kinds – from furniture to personal belongings – became larger and more ornate from the outset of the Victorian period until the reaction-styles set in at the end of the century. All this parallels the developments in the society and economy at large.

The increasing mechanization and industrialization of the country were also reflected in the making of furniture. Toward the end of the Empire period, furniture-making began its transition from individual craftsmen in workshops to an industry. Mechanization was already changing related domestic production industries. Machine-woven carpets and textiles for upholstery and wall-hangings were available as were roller-printed wallpaper, pattern-molded glass, and other machine-produced decoration. And this could not but affect the way furniture was designed and made. In his 1840 Baltimore publication, *The Cabinet Maker's Assistant*, John Hall wrote: 'Throughout the whole part of the designs in this work, particular attention has been bestowed in an economical arrangement to save labor; which being an important point, is presumed will render the collection exceedingly useful to the cabinet-maker.' The book was an illustration of the pillar-and-scroll style, which flowed out of the Greek-revival style practiced by Phyfe and

Right: The gothic style is evident in the shape and details of this side chair attributed to Alexander Jackson Davis.

others. In 1833, Joseph Meeks' Sons of New York, one of the leading furniture makers of the period, published an advertisement depicting 41 kinds of furniture all in the massive, flat-surfaced pillar-and-scroll style with its C-scroll and S-scroll supports – and all possible because of the new machinery that eliminated costly and time-consuming handwork.

In addition to developments in society at large affecting the making of furniture, there were more 'internal' forces changing the design of furniture. Several American architects, for instance, were fomenting a revolt against the Greek-revival house for which much of the Empire and related styles of furniture were being made. One of these was Andrew Jackson Downing (1815-1852), who called the houses of the prevailing style 'tasteless temples'; he preferred Gothic and gave his own Hudson River house a Gothic touch. Downing greatly influenced public taste after 1850 in another direction when he published *The Architecture of Country Houses* and encouraged the so-called 'cottage style'.

Another architect to take the lead in promoting the Gothic style was Thomas U Walter. In 1842, at the Franklin Institute's annual exhibition in Philadelphia, Walter, speaking for the judges, commended several Gothic pieces of furniture, including a sofa and chairs by C H and J F White. Walter called them a 'modified Gothic style which was a beautiful adaptation of that florid species of Architecture to furniture.' Then Walter issued the committee's warning against eclectic styles: 'it would be advisable for cabinetmakers generally to study greater simplicity in their designs; and when they adopt any particular style, to make every part of the work conform to it – the cultivated mind is always unpleasantly affected by a mixture of styles and orders.' This scolding was repeated throughout the Victorian period – and throughout the period happily went unheeded.

There are relatively few examples of pure Gothic domestic furniture. Most of the furniture was designed by architects who were building Gothic revival houses for the rich and designed furniture for those houses. The emphasis on vertical lines and elaborate ornamentation of the furniture clashed with a

The Library of the Colonel Robert J Milligan House, built in 1853, shows gothic detailing in the secretary, corner cupboard and chairs.

The elaborate carving of roses and cornucopiae is typical of John Henry Belter's work.

prevailing fondness for the horizontal lines emphasized in the Greek revival. The most famous designer of Gothic furniture which followed the more archaeological approach was Alexander Jackson Davis (1803-1892) of New York who designed Philip R Paulding's 'Lyndhurst' in Tarrytown, New York in 1841. Among the pieces of furniture he also designed for the house are a pair of rose-window-backed side chairs and a pedestal table.

The pure Gothic seemed more popularly relegated to public buildings: churches, libraries and colleges. For private consumption, it was not the style, but the motif that gained popularity. The result was Gothic ornamentation of classic Greek forms. Quatrefoils, trefoils, arches, steeple-turned finials, spandrels and other Gothic motifs can be found sprinkled through many styles, with the possible exception of the Rococo revival. It was this eclecticism which upset purists like the architect Thomas Walter.

By 1850 some significant changes were visible in the furniture business. 'Out West,'

Cincinnati, through its Chamber of Commerce, was claiming to be the 'largest furniture manufacturing city in America' with 136 establishments producing furniture valued at $1.6 million a year. John Broadfoot Smith employed 60 men and boasted production of almost 5000 tables, chairs and sofas in his factory in Cincinnati using steam-powered machines. This kind of competition was hard on the independent cabinetmaker, who was either forced out of business or forced into a factory. It was probably small consolation, but the skills of a cabinetmaker were still important, despite the increasing mechanization of the shops. The band-saw and fret-cutting machinery were available in 1850, although both continued to be perfected. The circular saw was in wide use at this time. It made cutting thin layers of wood for veneers quite easy, producing thinner and larger pieces.

The circular saw was a major influence on the furniture made by John Henry Belter in his New York factory, where he perfected laminating, bending, piercing and carving of rosewood to

A Belter couch with an armchair back of laminated rosewood, which was once owned by Abraham Lincoln.

make his name synonymous with Rococo revival. The Rococo revival, as a style, reinterpreted the original S-scrolls and serpentine lines with lacy borders of realistically carved fruits, flowers and even birds. Belter (1804-1863), a German immigrant, produced furniture of the Louis XV substyle, popular pieces like the sleigh bed, and innovations of his own like his curved-back side chairs. Belter developed, and patented, a way of forming two curves in the chairs, a concave back called 'dishing' and the S-curve seen by side silhouette.

All of Belter's furniture was made using his technological innovations in laminating and bending wood. Belter specialized in carved and pierced designs of grapes and vines and flowers. His veneer was always rosewood, a popular wood for this style because of its interesting grain and color.

In New Orleans, the immigrant Frenchman Prudent Mallard's work was popular. Mallard (1809-1879), also working in the eighteenth century Louis XV substyle, used rosewood and marble in his pieces. He was reputed to be the highest priced of the Southern cabinet makers, sometimes charging as much as $3000 for a bedroom set.

Several new forms appeared during the Rococo revival, including open-ended sofas, the *étagère*, and balloon-backed chairs. The *étagère* is simply an overgrown whatnot. It was meant to display *objets d'art* and souvenirs, and the desk was complicated to encourage careful examination of both the treasures and the piece by guests. The *étagère* was essentially a status symbol. Called a lady's chair by Victorians, the balloon-backed chair was shaped to complement the figure of a comely lady. The open-ended sofa sported coiled springs and down-filled pillows as well as a sinuous line emphasized by the carved wood frame.

Rococo revival furniture, with all its hand-carving and piercing, was expensive. New York's Charles A Baudouine, who infringed on Belter's patents, could get as much as $1200 for a set for the parlor. This put Rococo furniture beyond the means of all but the very rich. Middleclass Victorian Americans found a more

101

affordable and popular style in the so-called cottage furniture, which is part of the Elizabethan-revival style then popular.

In 1849, Sarah Josepha Hale, editor of *Godey's Lady's Book*, instituted a new feature, the 'Cottage Furniture Department.' The very next year, Andrew Jackson Downing – who was prominent in advancing the new Gothic style – published *The Architecture of Country Houses*, Both of these publications recommended cottage furniture as an alternative to the more expensive and taste-making styles of the day. Downing wrote, describing the furniture of Edward Hennessey of Boston: 'This furniture is remarkable for its combination of lightness and

The elaborate fretwork and marble shelf set off this rococo revival étagère by Roux.

strength, and for its essentially cottage-like character. It is very highly finished, and is usually painted drab, white, gray, a delicate lilac, or a fine blue – the surface polished and hard like enamel ... When it is remembered that the whole set for a cottage bedroom may be had for the price of a single wardrobe in mahogany, it will be seen how comparatively cheap it is.'

With such encouragement, the cottage style flourished. It was picked up by many of the midwestern factories which could make the furniture profitably – covering cheap wood, and often shoddy construction with layers of paint and stencil patterns. Well-made cottage furniture was bought by the rich for their summer 'cottages.' The middle classes satisfied themselves with the more mass-produced pieces.

Elizabethan revival furniture also meant spiral and spool-turned furnishings. The spiral-turned chairs of this period often used Gothic motifs and were called Gothic by Victorians; Downing however, refers to the style as Elizabethan. The spool-turned ornamentation of chairs, beds, tables and whatnots was popular in country styles, and easily produced in factories. The spool-turned furniture remained popular throughout the century.

The Renaissance and Louis XVI revivals are sometimes described as interchangable, reflecting a taste for the more massive ornamentation over the intricate ornmentation of the previous styles. Both, as their names suggest, were heavily influenced by European models. Leon Marcotte, who arrived in New York in 1854 from France, was one of the most successful makers of the Renaissance Revival style. This style was characterized by 'Pompeian' turned legs, arched pediments, and bold rectangular lines often incised with gilt. In an 1860 advertisement, Marcotte was selling 'Very rich suites in Blackwood and Gilt, covered in Moire Antique ... Black and Gilt Centre Tables with very rich Gilt Bronzes; etc.' This is a very French representation of the Rennaissance style. American furniture manufactories were also offering Renaissance work. In Cincinnati, the firm of Mitchell and Rammelsberg, which started in 1844, had grown to become the largest furniture business in the United States. They offered a secretary-bookcase, in what was probably considered the Renaissance style. Its large massive lines and deep carving reflect not so much the French style, as a more typical mid-Victorian style suitable for the brownstone town houses of the era. In Grand Rapids, the Berkey & Gay Furniture Company exhibited an elaborate jasper-topped and walnut veneered Renaissance bedroom suite at the Philadelphia Centennial Exposition in 1876. Although it excited favorable public comment, the architects, again, were dismayed yet hopeful that 'such an array of vulgarity in design as emanated from the thriving city of Grand Rapids will never again bring disgrace upon the American name at an international exhibition.'

By the time her husband, Napoleon III, had been deposed in 1870, Empress Eugenie's taste for Louis XVI furniture had established itself in America. The style is similar to the Renaissance with its incised gilt lines on dark or ebonized wood. Some of the pieces, true to the French influence, have Egyptian ornamentation reflecting the recent construction of the Suez Canal. One such center table, made in New York, possibly by Marcotte, has a porcelain plaque of the sphinx in the center of the skirt. Each of the four ebonized and gilted legs is topped with carved masks. The incised gilt lines are geometric, also reflecting the Egyptian influence.

The best practitioners of this style, with its porcelain plaques, ormolu mounts, gold leaf and wood inlays, were probably the immigrant

Charles Beaudoine used rosewood laminate on a pair of cardtables made in 1852.

Left and below: *Victorian side chairs might be simply carved with caned seats, or pierced rosewood laminate upholstered in Brussels carpet.*

cabinetmakers who learned their craft in France, Germany and England. The Germans, particularly, had good reputations as carvers – such craftsmen as George H Hankel of Philadelphia, the Herter Brothers of New York, and Henry Weil in New Orleans.

The Louis XVI revival was essentially an East Coast phenomenon. The taste for such richly ornamented, expensive furniture led one prominent social critic to comment that it 'was well suited to the frivolities of the life too frequently led nowadays by the extraordinarily wealthy.'

Eugenie's influence was more profoundly felt in the direction of collecting and in the Victorian idea of decorating rooms than through her taste in furniture. She was fond of comfort, and cherished an affinity with Marie Antoinette. One French visitor to her rooms later wrote: 'The suite of the Empress consists of two

rooms united by a sort of arcade – a dream . . . Paintings, Flowers, artistic treasures, little corners, niches, retreats, grottoes concealed by drapery behind screens of foliage and flowers, with lamps among the branches.' Her revolutionary scheme of interior decoration went further. Eugenie introduced *confortables*: large settees, easy chairs, ottomans and pouffes, all thickly padded and upholstered with wood showing. The richness of her court, to which many wealthy Americans were welcome, set a high standard for emulation.

Her interest in 'artistic treasures' encouraged art collecting among rich Americans, many of whom had flocked to Paris for the 1867 Exposition. The wealth of these visitors is hard to underestimate. An 1863 letter to the Cincinnati Chamber of Commerce disclosed, 'The whole people in the Loyal States are rich beyond their anticipation and they feel it, and are extravagant beyond precedence. Again, in 1865, 'Furniture: During the past year furniture dealers saw their customers selecting Tables and Chairs, Book Cases, Bedsteads, and Sofas, not because of their intrinsic beauty, but because they cost round sums. High prices were an inducement and prices were much higher than ever before.' As one example, Cornelius Vanderbilt's fortune, made on railroads, was estimated at about one hundred million dollars by 1870.

The Empress and her lovely city certainly 'induced' an interest in culture, a word that gained importance in the 1870s. The seed was sown for annual pilgrimages to Europe to collect art and antiques. In June 1873, George Templeton Strong wrote in his diary: 'Visited this afternoon the Metropolitan Museum of Art in the late Mrs Douglas Cruger's palazzo on West Fourteenth Street. ... Art treasures (so called) are evidently accumulating in New York, being picked up in Europe by all our millionaires and brought home. The collection promises very well indeed.' This interest in collecting art coincided with the beginnings of Impressionist painting. Perhaps this is one reason that the Impressionism collections in American museums are so fine.

The English had not had a major influence on American furniture styles since the days of

One of Belter's masterpieces is a pierced and carved bed of laminated rosewood.

Sheraton and Hepplewhite. But at the Philadelphia Exhibition in 1876, Norman Shaw, a British architect, tried to introduce what was called a Queen Anne style of furniture. The style was based on principles of William Morris' Arts and Crafts movement, then gaining popularity in England. This was not only a movement back to simplicity, but also a movement back to hand-crafted furniture. It wasn't the right time. Harriet Spofford wrote in 1878: 'The Queen Anne met with opposition and allegation that the Pre-Raphaelites had made it up; it seems to be the very style to reward the search of the nineteenth century for something natural, beautiful, suitable and convenient.' One other of Shaw's ideas did catch on, though – the English style of Queen Anne houses.

In American minds, this may have reminded them of the Empress Eugenie's rooms with their conversation areas and grottoes, for most of the architects, like their American clients, were still captivated by things French. Shaw advocated an open downstairs; a style called 'Free Classic,' in which there are no rooms, no doors. The idea caught on in the 1880s and open spaces were subdivided by arches, pillars and woodwork screening. Cozy corners were established, and beautifully carved woodwork became fashionable.

The trend horrified American novelist Edith Wharton. In her book *The Decoration of Houses*,

Left: *The elaborate carving of the furniture in the Belter Parlour at the Metropolitan Museum of Art in New York stands in high contrast to the equally popular spool furniture like the table seen below.*

Despite the elaborate carving, this Belter bureau shows a pleasing balance and symmetry.

Wharton's book, published in 1897, was just one voice toward the end of this era which was calling for a return to stylistic integrity: 'Architecture and decoration ... [has] wandered since 1800 in a labyrinth of dubious eclecticism. ... The decorator of the present day may be compared to a person who is called upon to write a letter in the English language, but is ordered, in so doing, to conform to Chinese or Egyptian rules of grammar, or possibly both together.'

The separation of tasks found in factory-produced furniture seems evident in this secretary bookcase made by Mitchell and Rammelsberg in Cincinnati, Ohio.

which she wrote with architect Ogden Codman Jr, Mrs Wharton stressed the need for doors to allow privacy and order. She wrote: 'English taste has never been so sure as that of the Latin races; and it has moreover, been perpetually modified by a passion for contriving all kinds of supposed "conveniences," which instead of simplifying life not infrequently tend to complicate it. Americans have inherited this trait, and in both countries the architect or upholsterer who can present a new and more intricate way of planning a house or of making a piece of furniture, is more sure of a hearing than he who follows the accepted lines.'

In the 1880s, although wicker bedroom furniture was being produced *en suite*, suites were generally not used in downstairs rooms of the well-to-do. Occasionally a few basic pieces had matching frames, but the upholstery was not always in matching fabric. Gypsy and occasional tables upholstered with fringes were popular as were Turkish ottomans. The Morris chair appeared, an indication of a coming interest in simpler lines. Meanwhile, the pervasive American tendency to choose from a whole smorgasbord of styles continued throughout the Victorian Age, with an almost dazzling variety of types of styles of furniture popular at various times or among various groups of Americans.

Interest in the Orient developed in America following the viewing of the Japanese Bazaar at the 1876 Philadelphia Centennial Exhibition. Prior to the exhibition, the major oriental influence had been a process called japanning. This coating and decorating of wood with lacquer or enamel was borrowed by European craftsmen and then Americans, but Westerners never had the materials to properly emulate the process.

Immediately after the Exhibition, popular demand for the light, airy Oriental furniture had to be satisfied by importing objects from Hong Kong and other Eastern ports. Soon, though, American factories geared up to produce furniture with an Oriental air. Sometimes the materials were imported, but it was cheaper to treat birdseye maple to resemble bamboo. Hand-painted Japanese tiles became popular; they were incorporated into furniture as well as used for decoration on floors, walls, ceilings, fireplaces and bathrooms.

Herter Brothers of Philadelphia was one of the first to incorporate tiles in their furniture in 1876. Kilian Brothers of New York manufactured imitation bamboo furniture during the same time. By the 1880s furniture companies everywhere were making Oriental-style furniture. The list includes: Ardi of Grand Rapids, New York and Hong Kong; A Meinecke & Son of Milwaukee; the Nimura and Sato Company of Brooklyn; and J E Hall of Boston.

A taste for Turkish furniture came to America via England and France. The French picked up the new style from their travels in the Ottoman Empire while building the Suez Canal between 1859 and 1869. By the 1870s, overstuffed armchairs, ottomans, daybeds and sofas were

The bureau incorporating a full-length mirror became popular in the 1870s.

present in many well-to-do American Victorian homes.

Turkish furniture was entirely covered with fine fabrics, tapestry, silk brocades, velours and leather. Coil springs were used for extra comfort and beaded fringes added for decoration. Furniture of this sort was also manufactured by factories in Grand Rapids and sold through various outlets, like the Sears and Roebuck catalog which offered Turkish furnishing for 'unprecedented comfort' at a price more affordable to the growing middle class. For those interested in a simpler style, there were alternatives. Lambert Hitchcock opened his cabinet and chair factory in 1818 in Barkhamsted, Connecticut to build chair parts and send them

south and west where they were put together and sold. The business flourished, becoming one of the leading industries in the town. By 1825, Hitchcock decided to manufacture whole chairs and ship them out in the same manner. Requiring more space for this venture, he built a three-story brick factory to employ more than one hundred men, women and children. The village that sprang up around his factory was named Hitchcocksville; today it is called Riverton.

Hitchcock participated in a revolution in cabinet making – the factory production of furniture. In his factory, men ran water-powered saws and children painted the chairs, while women applied the stencils. The factory was, therefore, an early experiment in mass production.

Hitchcock chairs were made of birch or maple and first painted red by children. A coat of black was laid over the red for a rosewood effect. The women applied stenciled designs with their fingers, which they first dipped in oil, then dry bronze or gold powder and rubbed across the stencil. The color of the fruit, flowers or birds was then applied with a brush. The factory made straight chairs and Salem rockers as well as other styles.

In 1829, a victim of his own success, Hitchcock was forced into bankruptcy, but was saved from failure by the man who was about to become his brother-in-law, Arba Alford Jr. Hitchcock was producing and selling plenty of chairs, but his prices were so low, $1.50 a chair, that his net income was sustained only by high production. Unfortunately, he became the victim of what we today call an over-stocked inventory. At the time, transportation systems were not well enough established to make shipping easy. He had several thousand chairs in stock and with his agents. One result of the reorganization was a raise in price by twenty-five cents. Hitchcock, being one of the first such manufacturers in America, was also one of the first to come upon such problems of profit margin, shipping constraints, and later in his life, competition from other manufactories of painted chairs.

He died in 1856, but some 90 years later John T Kenney opened a chair factory in the same building to manufacture Hitchcock Chairs

Left: *Unusual woods such as sycamore became popular in the later nineteenth century.*

Above: *Small marble-top tables on walnut frames were popular throughout the period.*

again. The modern Hitchcock Chair Company was founded in 1946; the first order, for 150 chairs, was delivered in November 1948. The company is still in business in Riverton today.

British travelers in the United States in the 1830s noted the American love affair with rocking chairs in such a way to suggest these chairs would not be found in a proper British household. Miss Harriet Martineau wrote: 'In the Inn parlors are three or four rocking chairs in which sit ladies who are vibrating in different directions and at varying velocities, so as to try the head of a stranger ... How this lazy and ungraceful indulgence ever became general, I cannot imagine; but the nation seems so wedded to it that I see little chance of its being forsaken.' Miss Martineau also noted that when American ladies travel to Europe they, 'sometimes send home for a rocking chair.'

The opening of the Suez Canal in 1869 gave rise to the popularity of ancient Egyptian motifs.

Until the 1800s, most rocking chairs were made-over straightback chairs to which rockers were added, usually windsors, slatback or banister back chairs. About 1825, chairmakers began taking the style seriously, producing rocking chairs from their shops. As rocking chairs gained in popularity, the form flourished through many variations.

In Boston, the seat was reshaped to curve upward in the back and down in the front, like an S, offering more support for the spine and a gentler edge for the knees. The Boston Rocker, as it is called, was probably one of the most popular chairs ever built. Its fame spread quickly throughout the rest of the country. Its style was copied by other manufacturers who proudly offered rocking chairs 'of the Boston pattern.'

For a time the chair was thought as suitable only for women, children and the elderly. Part of its enduring popularity results from the social acceptance of the chair for all ages, both sexes, and eventually in any room of the house. Many early forms of the chair, like the rocking Windsor settee with a removeable fence, were designed with women in mind. The settee allowed a mother to rock her infant at her side, freeing her hands for mending or other chores. Rocking potty chairs were built for children, with the chamber pot secured underneath a cushion when it was not needed.

In the 1830s William Hancock, of Boston, manufactured and upholstered, spring-seated rocking chairs with jigsaw-cut scrolled arms and expensive button upholstery. This development of the platform rocker signals the movement of the chair into the Victorian parlor. This larger, more masculine style also indicates the beginning acceptance by vigorous Victorian men of 'rocking chairs.'

The innovations of the nineteenth century – the Boston rocker, windsor-style, or Salem rocker and the platform rocker – are today classic forms.

In 1774, responding to a divine call, Ann Lee, her brother William, and seven other members of the Shaker community in England boarded the ship *Mariah* and came to America. Mother Ann, as she was called, founded the Shaker community in this country, where it flourished after several years of hardship and spread from New York into New England and the Midwest.

By 1789, Shakers were successfully producing chairs for community use and for sale. A chair

Right: *The Renaissance revival cabinet made use of various materials including inlays and bronze.*
Below: *Porcelain plaques decorated in the style of Louis XIV were also used in 'French cabinets.'*

Left: *Needlework was a popular seat covering, especially on small chairs and footstools.*
Above: *The popular Hitchcock rocker was available in several different designs.*

factory in Mt Lebanon, the largest settlement, located in eastern New York state, mass-produced chairs bearing the Mt Lebanon stencil. The dominant traits of those chairs, as with all Shaker furniture, were simplicity and utility.

From about 1800 to 1850, almost 5000 men, women and children joined the United Society of Believers in Christ's Second Appearing for a peak population of over 6000 members in 20 communities by 1860. The Shakers were a separatist and communal society whose members devoted their lives to the second coming of Christ. Individuality and personal pride were consecrated to the greater good – devotion to the pure life of Christ. Shaker craftsmen were

guided by their religious principles and the Millennial Laws in making furniture and other goods for the communities in New England, New York, Ohio, Indiana and Kentucky.

The craftsmen developed a style uniquely inspired by the needs of the community and the bond in Christ that brought them together. 'Anything may with strict propriety, be called perfect which perfectly answers the purpose for which it was designed': this view of the Millennial Church was echoed in all phases of Shaker life.

The Laws dictated how the houses would be furnished – bedsteads were painted green, bed-spreads and wall hangings should be blue and

Above: *Rocking chairs were frequently upholstered to give greater comfort to the elderly and invalids. This one was made in the 1830s.*
Below left: *The Hitchcock side-chair was decorated with gilded stencils.*

white, but not checked or striped. Only one rocking chair was allowed in the dormitories unless an elderly person resided there; the elderly were allowed the comfort of their own rocking chairs.

Traditional Shaker furniture was not upholstered, only lightly varnished, or painted. Set in simple rooms with white walls and varnished uncurtained windows, the furniture was simple, with a style in which everything was devoted to simplicity, and superfluity was associated with sinfulness. Materials were pared down to only what was needed – posts of large chairs, for example, were only one-inch thick, and some of the rockers on rocking chairs

THE HITCHCOCK CHAIR COMPANY
Riverton (Hitchcocks-ville) Connecticut

Above: *Suites of furniture were made especially for the parlor.*
Below: *Abraham Lincoln owned this comfortable buttonback rocker.*

were not more than a half inch thick. The dining tables were made of a pine board supported on two slender pedestals. Instead of the traditional stretcher that supplied additional support, Shakers used diagonal iron struts which allowed for more leg room.

After the Civil War, the number of converts dropped off. Many communities, especially those which supported themselves by farming, began failing. By 1875, the community was listed at 2500 members and by 1900 it was a mere 1000. The advent of machines and factories left Shaker craftsmen, with the apparent exception of the Mt Lebanon community, unable to compete. One sign of the disintegration within the communities was an increased interest in comfort and embellishment.

Today, over two hundred years later, it is easy to recognize the joyous spirit which permeates their work. Rather than stifling creativity, the exacting commands of simplicity and utility seemed to free the craftsmen's spirits to the production of truly beautiful work. In the quiet lines and gentle sheen of Shaker furniture the unity of spiritual and secular worlds is revealed. The evidence of secular activities guided by the wisdom of the spirit is expressed in the Shaker proverb: 'Every force evolves a form.'

At the opposite side of the continent, pioneer craftsmen settling the frontiers of the southwest came under the strong, often geometric, Spanish and Native American influence. Indications of the Southwest influence are found in the square stiles – often with notched

Above: *The pharmacy at Hancock Shaker Village contains a massive chest in the Shaker style and a table with proportionally fine legs.*
Below: *Additions to furniture in the nurse shop made the beds more comfortable for the patients.*

finials and solid rectangular seats – that extended beyond the legs in some of the better-made furniture. Materials used were different; rawhide was woven for seats, and Western yellow pine, juniper and cottonwood were often used for construction.

The Native American influence is seen in so-called Mission Chairs, heavy chairs with square stiles, often rawhide upholstering and crests of jagged design. Many of these chairs were made by members of the tribe for priests in the missions, thus their name. Sometimes the squared posts were curved at the back to accommodate the human body more comfortably; often, then, the arms of the chairs will repeat the curve.

This style would be taken up and developed later in the century in reaction to the shoddy construction and overblown detail that was the culmination of mid-nineteenth-century furniture.

Not everyone throughout America was in a position to purchase furniture in a shop or have a craftsman's custom design. Many pioneers had to rely on their own ingenuity and skill or on that of a neighbor to furnish their homes. Country furniture, then, refers to that furniture that was made by individuals for their own or local use and made from materials available in their environment.

Often popular styles in the furniture centers of Boston, New York, Philadelphia and Baltimore, would filter westward and be reflected in country workshops as much as ten years later. The rural craftsman had to adapt forms to the demands of a harsher environment than experienced by city folk. Sometimes furniture had to be invented where there was nothing to suit the purpose.

While high-posted canopied beds were fashionable in the more settled homes, one found low-posted beds in rural houses where the rooms were smaller and the ceilings, especially upstairs, not so high. The low-posted Jenny Lind bed with spool-turned posts was a style popular in country houses, along with beds with cannonball posts. Low-posted beds were easier to make, too. The Jenny Lind beds were among the first to use slats instead of lacings to hold the mattresses. Early (1830s) spool-turned beds had straight lines, while the later beds, made after 1850, had curved corners on the headboards and footboards. The Jenny Lind beds were among the first to use countersunk screws in construction. The name was given to

Huge buffets or commodes were primarily ornamental.

Above: *Southwestern furniture showed great Spanish influence and was entirely handworked before 1840.* Right: *Furniture made at the utopian settlement at Zoar, Ohio, imitated the characteristic German styles of the immigrants.*

these spool-turned beds after a shrewd Philadelphia cabinetmaker gave Jenny Lind a spool-turned bed during her American tour in 1850; this association may also account for the enduring popularity of the style.

One of the most famous styles of country furniture is the rocking chair which was found at the hearth and on the porch of many small houses. It was important for the woman with babies to nurse, peas to shell and clothes to mend: a comfortable setting for such unending chores. Ladderback and slatback chairs were popular and gradually modified. As more were made, the backs became shorter until soon the ladderbacks comprised only two slats. Chair seats in the South and West were often built of available materials. In the South, corn husks were woven for seats instead of using rushes. In the West rawhide thong seats were made. The Shakers used a special tape woven on narrow looms. This type of tape was also sold outside their communities.

Settlers faced the problems of traveling into the wilderness with an ingenuity which often resulted in new forms of furniture, like the wagonseat chair. The driver needed a seat that was high enough to see ahead, and narrow

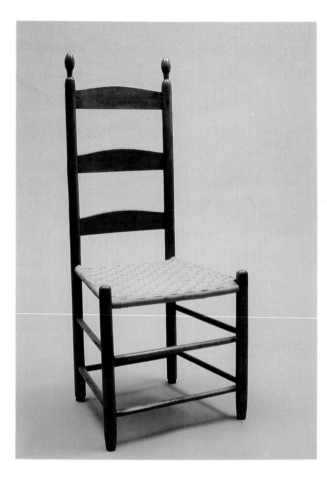

Above: *The most familiar Shaker chairs had rush or taped seats; the tape seat was a particular Shaker favorite.*

Below: *A maple and pine bench designed and constructed by members of the utopian colony at Aurora, Oregon.*

Above: *The Shaker belief in things 'plain and simple' is evident in the design and execution of this child's high chair.*

Above: *The Shaker settlement at Mount Lebanon, New York, was famous for its chairs, including this swivel design.*

enough to fit in the bed of the wagon. Settlers built a settee with short legs and slat back that could be removed from the wagon and carried into a meeting house or the new house.

Earlier in the seventeenth century, the need for space had resulted in development of the chair-table. When not needed, the table-top was raised, the piece pushed against the wall to serve as a chair; raised, the table top protected the seater from drafts. This form was built and used until the late nineteenth century. Tables which also served as chests and benches, called hutch or settle tables, were made for ultimate utility as late as 1880. When not needed as a table, the top raised revealing a bench whose seat could be raised for storage of blankets and other property.

One other style was developed by country furniture-makers: the schoolmaster's desk. This tall-legged desk had a sloping top that could be raised, revealing a compartment for

books, an inkwell and a pencil tray. Some of them had a drawer, most were plainly built. They were used both in school houses and small business offices. So far as is known, the schoolmaster's desk was never made by a city cabinetmaker or in a factory, making it a true piece of country furniture.

Wicker furniture came to America on the *Mayflower*. There is a wicker cradle in Pilgrim Hall at Plymouth, Massachusetts which rocked Peregrine White to sleep after he was born on shipboard in 1620.

The term wicker refers to a flexible shoot, like willow, rattan, or red, which was woven for baskets and furniture. This pliant material made possible designs which would show off fancy work. The open work of weaving was cooler than wooden chairs, and the material responded to the body, much the way a good leather shoe will mold to the contours of the individual foot.

A bed from New Mexico

The style first became popular as porch furniture in the mid-1800s. When wicker moved indoors it was in reaction to the heavy cast-iron furniture and the dark interiors of the 1890 Victorian house. Cast-iron mirror frames were replaced by bamboo and rattan frames. The plant stand, a form of *étagère* which became popular in the nineteenth century also metamorphosed into lighter rattan and bamboo forms. These were long-legged affairs with a gallery to keep the potted plant from falling and a second shelf for holding the watering can. There were wicker magazine stands, wicker tables for serving lemonade, and rattan chaises longues.

Bamboo was used to make accessory furnishings, for example hall stands with two shelves and a mirror. Calling cards, hats and pocketbooks could be left on the shelves while the caller checked his or her appearance in the mirror. For less formal rooms of the home, sun rooms and bedrooms, wicker was painted green or white, or varnished. Chairs were made with legs in the Louis XV fashion, high and gently curved. Frames of hickory or white oak were wrapped with steamed and woven cane. Rattan and bamboo bookshelves were often varnished and decorated with Japanese laquerwork on the doors.

At the other end of the scale, the heavy Woo-

ton desk embodies one of our assumptions about Victorian America with its imposing exterior which opens to dozens of compartments designed for organization and privacy. The desk was invented, designed, patented and manufactured in Indianapolis between 1875 and 1884 by William S Wooton, a Quaker.

Wooton actually made four grades of desk to suit the needs of every businessman. They ranged in price from $90 to $750 for Ordinary Grade, Standard Grade, Extra-Grade, and Superior-Grade. The largest desk (Superior-Grade) was patented first as a 'Cabinet Office Secretary,' and was constructed of black walnut with French polished exotic veneers. Berlin bronze hardware was used on all the grades of

A trastero *or cupboard from New Mexico reveals the through-tenon joinery which gives the piece a seventeenth-century quality.*

desks for heavy cast hinges, door handles and letter slots.

By 1876 Wooton had a world market for his desks, in part because of his show at the Centennial Exhibition in Philadelphia. In 1884, the London *Graphic* noted: 'One hundred and ten compartments, all under one lock and key. A place for everything and everything in its place. Order Reigns Supreme, Confusion Avoided. Time Saved. Vexation Spared.... Nothing in its line can exceed it in usefulness or beauty, and purchasers everywhere express themselves delighted with its manifold convenience.' Wooton's desks were sold by agents in cities across the United States as well as in London, Glasgow, and Rio de Janeiro. In America, the desk was owned by such prominent men as John D Rockefeller, Joseph Pulitzer, Jay Gould and Ulysses S Grant.

The proportions of the Superior-Grade desk are imposing. It was six feet tall, almost four feet wide, and about three feet deep. The two front sections swung open to reveal the compartments for filing books, papers, letters and other paraphernalia. A drop-front writing table, when lowered, revealed yet more compartments.

Folding chairs are almost as old as furniture. In twelfth-century Europe, when the nobility moved from castle to castle frequently, many of their chairs were actually what we would call stools. They called them *pliants* and they collapsed for easy moving. Mobility among the

A campaign table used by Rutherford B Hayes during the Civil War folds up to provide a carrying case.

upper class was such a fact of life that the Spanish (*muebles*), French (*meubles*) and Italian (*mobili*) word for furniture means movables.

The proliferation of chairs, as Americans came to know them, didn't occur until they settled down and transportation became easier. Folding chairs, in the nineteenth century, were made for easy storage, and ease in shipment. Thus they were excellent furniture to use on campaigns during the Civil War. While most campaign furniture was wood, metal chairs (and beds) were also constructed for use by

A wicker-work settee which includes gothic arches in its design was made for Samuel Colt of Hartford.

Norwegian immigrants built furniture similar to that which they had known at home.
The design of the kubbestol, *or log chair, is unchanged from the Middle Ages.*

officers in the Civil War, unfortunately we don't have details about their manufacture. Few examples of these mobile camp furnishings have survived or been found, but they are frequently seen in photographs.

Collignon Brothers Manufactories of Closter, New Jersey, specialized in manufacturing folding chairs, including folding rocking chairs, which were sold in their showrooms in New York City. In 1876, two brothers, Adam and Claudius Collignon patented their Grecian-shaped rocker noting, 'A rocking-chair with arms, as ordinarily constructed, is cumbersome and unwieldy to move from place to place. . . . When shipped, rocking chairs occupy much valuable space that might otherwise be saved. To obviate these disadvantages we construct our arm rocking-chair so that it may be folded into a compact shape, occupying comparatively little space, and admitting of its easy transportation.' In 1881, alone, at least seven patents were issued for rocking chairs that folded in a variety of ways.

There were also made, in factories, uphol-stered camp chairs with the traditional X-shaped supports that crossed at the seat. The back and seat of this chair, which could be fitted with rockers, was upholstered; the rails were covered with material. The arms were uphol-stered slings. The type of chair was made by numerous factories in varying designs. Black walnut, cherry and oak were the common wood and sometimes maple or birch were used, but usually these were ebonized. The upholstery was either tapestry or similar material. These chairs, made between 1870 and 1885, could be brought out-of-doors at the summer cottages of the well-to-do.

The term 'easy chairs' originally referred to chairs for invalids and the term was used into the nineteenth century. What are called easy chairs today were called at that time 'lolling chairs,' calling to mind the phrase, 'lolling around.'

The easy chairs were upholstered with high backs and wings so if one had the strength to get out of bed, one could sit near a fire or gazing out the window while protected from drafts and well supported. Many easy chairs had chamber pots secured under a removable seat cushion as a further convenience for those in ill health. The stylistic details were adapted to the fashion of the time.

With all the developments in gadgetry, machinery, and 'science' in the mid- to late-nineteenth century, invalid chairs flourished. As might be expected, the rocking chair was prime for development for the invalid: 'The Health Jolting Chair ... The most important Health Mechanism ever produced. It Preserves Health, Cures Disease, and Prolongs Life.' It also sold for $35 in George Sander's New York catalog in 1890. This rocking chair was built with a set of spring mechanisms between the seat and the legs, instead of rockers. It was an exercise chair; popping up and down in the chair directed blood to the right places, 'the Essentially Nutritive Organs of the Body.' This

Above: *A primitive field desk used by Rutherford B Hayes during the Civil War.*

Below: *A walnut desk built by an immigrant, Elias Hanson, in Iowa in 1870 is similar to Norwegian furniture built earlier in the century.*

and other similar devices would refresh the brain, ease constipation, torpid livers, nervous prostration, loss of appetite and corpulency. They were advertised for the blind, insane, aged, weak, crippled, convalescent, and 'sedentary consumers,' particularly intellectuals. Other rockers patented at this time were specifically called 'invalid chairs' and featured the ability to support a reclining patient.

There also developed, in 1865, an anti-rocker rocker called, 'The True Physiological Chair' which had a fifth leg and a short seat. This chair, advertised in *Health Tract No 13*, was an antidote to 'the unwieldy and disease engendering rocking-chair' specifically for consumptives and those with spinal deformities. The chair, and its unknown inventor, sought to preserve the human form as 'our Maker intended it' with an erect back. If one slouched in the chair, with its eight-inch-long seat, one would fall out of it.

Most of the invalid chairs patented were more conservative in both claim and design. C B Sheldon patented his reclining upholstered chair in 1876. The frame was made of cast iron and walnut. The chair, which was produced by Marks A F Chair Company of New York, could be reclined to become a bed by means of a rachet device under the arms. One piece, featured in the *The Cabinet Maker's Assistant* published in Baltimore in 1840, was an adaptation of the Voltaire chair into an invalid chair.

The Wooton patent desk, with open doors revealing the filing drawers, writing surface, and necessary heavy brass hinges.

Le Voltaire, as it was called, was a popular lolling chair with its open arms, low seat and high contoured back in the French Restoration style. Hall adapted the chair so the back 'can be varied at pleasure and the projecting part in the front can be elongated and adjusted at any angle to the seat.'

Another innovation of the nineteenth century was the imaginative use of material. Metal has been used in furniture for centuries. During the Renaissance, Italian and Spanish artisans made furnishings from wrought iron. By about 1825, in England and France, blacksmiths produced wrought iron garden furniture. Within 15 years, by 1840, iron garden furniture was fashionable in America. On this side of the Atlantic, however, the furniture was made from cast, not wrought, iron.

The change is indicative of the mass pro-

duction strategies which had become important to economic survival. Cast-iron furniture was made in foundries with sand molds; wooden patterns were pressed into the sand, removed, and molten metal was poured in. The pieces were put together with iron bolts. Many of the patterns were similar, thanks, in part, to the publication of a pattern book by Robert Woods, of Philadelphia, in 1840. The furniture was too heavy to be shipped at a reasonable cost but, being new, it was the latest vogue, and customers could be found everywhere. By the 1860s, foundries were making cast-iron furniture all over the country, as far west as California.

Garden furniture was styled after the romantic view of wild, untended gardens fashionable on either side of the Atlantic. Grape clusters, ferns, lilies of the valley and scrolls were motifs for circular settees on goats' feet from the center of which sprouted an ersatz tree trunk. The furniture was painted yearly to deter rust.

The market for cast-iron furniture expanded when foundries started casting indoor furniture about 1855. One theory has it that the indoor cast-iron furniture was the working man's answer to the more expensive Louis XV-Rococo style currently popular. Thus the indoor furniture was designed with those details in mind. It was painted black, with gilt, or in colors simulating rosewood or black walnut. Foundries in virtually every state and territory turned out coat racks, umbrella stands, parlor tables, mirror frames, fire screens, plant stands, and bedsteads decorated in foliage and curlicues.

The cast-iron beds were perhaps the most graceful examples of this exuberance, and they gained enduring popularity. The head and foot board were identical, 34 to 38 inches tall with elaborate open scroll work perched on short cabriole legs. The pattern of C- and S-scrolls often centered around lyres or circular medallions. The beds were six feet four inches long by three feet six inches wide. They are considered forerunners of the iron and brass beds which become popular at the turn of the century.

Improvements in wire, developed for the laying of the transatlantic telegraph cable in the 1850s, yielded yet another material for furniture-makers – a strong but flexible wire. The result is the popular ice cream parlor chair and table, as well as wire plant stands.

Another form of furniture popular between 1840 and 1870, was papier-mâché, made in England by Jennen and Bettridge of Birmingham. The American center for this durable, feather-light, furniture was Litchfield, Connecticut. Only a small number of full-scale furnishing items are said to have been made there, however.

Papier-mâché furniture, another indication of the inventive attitude towards materials and furniture in the late nineteenth century, was made by pressing paper pulp and strips of paper mixed with glue under great pressure. Black lacquer and gilt patterns were used to finish the pieces.

Chairs other than garden furniture might have iron frames. This is an early example of the cantilever principle.

Several patents were issued in America for this process. One, in 1772, was issued to a Henry Clay for molding pasted sheets of soft porous paper in ovens set at 1100°F. The shaped form was immersed in various solutions and baked again at 200°F before being lacquered and decorated. A second patent, in 1825, was granted for inlaying mother-of-pearl. The most popular chairs made of papier-mâché were balloon-backed on U-shaped seats with cabriole legs.

It is important to recognize that virtually all of these styles were being produced in the United States between 1840 and 1870 with varying degrees of popularity. Since suites of furniture were just becoming popular, one could still find in many parlors a Rococo *étagère*, a set of spiral-turned Elizabethan side chairs and perhaps one of Joseph Meeks heavy scroll-style center tables. One is most likely to find a deliberate unity of style in houses where architects had also designed furniture to match the architectural style of the house. This proliferation of styles probably reflects the exuberance of such times when inventions and innovations made so many techniques simpler, at least from the cabinetmaker's point of view. For the public, the American Industrial Revolution offered prosperity to many, and given the newness of 'things,' this was best reflected materially.

Census figures from 1880 give us an indication of just how large the furniture industry had grown: There were a reported 4843 furniture factories and 384 chair shops which employed

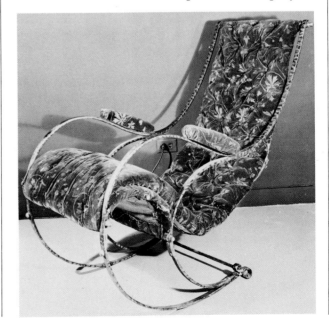

Above: *The grape design was a popular pattern in cast-iron garden furniture.*
Below: *Flexible wire was used for plant stands and garden furniture.*

53,018 men over the age of 16; 2216 women over the age of 15 and 3068 children. The annual value of furniture produced by these businesses totaled 77.8 million dollars. Significant quantities of American furniture were being shipped to foreign countries like Australia and the many nations in South America were also customers.

The rapid industrialization was aided by continued development in technology and required the separation of art from industry. Producing furniture was now a matter of distinct tasks, no longer was an artisan required with his complete knowledge of woods and techniques. Itinerant workers had at their disposal scrapers, molders, band and scroll saws, wood polishing machines, planers, carvers, grinders, benders and wood-engraving machines. By the 1870s, mass production in factories had progressed to the point that the man who did the case work, in the example of a secretary-bookcase, and the man who carved the ornament were not the same. It would have

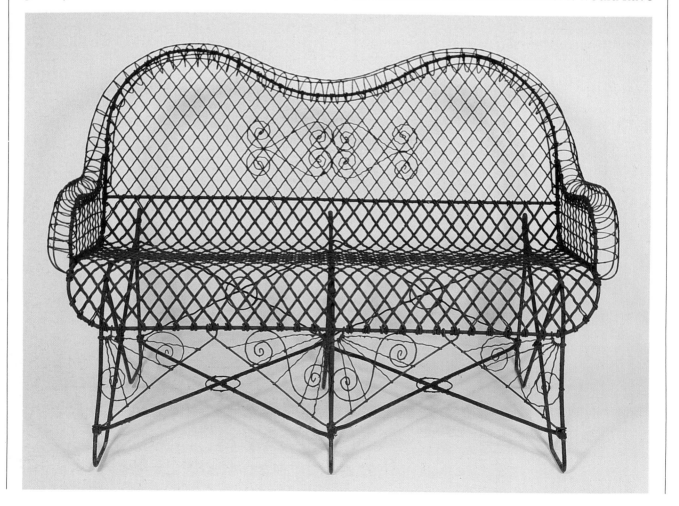

been inefficient to have one man doing both. The result is an unfortunate disintegration in design integrity, which in the finer pieces was, however, only readily apparent to the most critical eye.

These companies, and this process of industrialization, made possible a level of convenience and luxury undreamed of before. If Victorian Americans were confusing gadgetry and convenience with civilization as they were accused by de Toqueville, it is not hard to understand how and why. Many Americans of the 1880s were still familiar with the conditions they left behind in beloved homelands to emigrate to this 'land of opportunity.' In a little more than one hundred years, Americans had fought four major wars to secure their country, crossed hundreds of miles of unexplored land to settle their country, and fought numerous fierce skirmishes and battles to wrest the land from the Native Americans who knew it to be their home.

The attempt here is not to issue a moral judgment, but to evoke the unself-conscious, self-absorbed determined effort to thrive. After all, criticism of the luxuries and comforts available to the greater population came primarily from two quarters: the wealthy, educated, cultivated thinkers, and those by whose labor the material comforts were made possible, but who were not able to enjoy them. But all this was part of the fast-changing nineteenth-century American world, a society as exuberant and eclectic and contradictory as its furniture.

The sitting room of Olana, Frederic Church's country house, shows the move away from the overstuffed opulence of the middle of the century.

5
Seeking New Forms
1876-1929

In the nineteenth century taste was not linear in development. All major nineteenth century styles coexisted throughout the century, and American catalogs of the early 1900s offered furniture in styles originated in the 1840s. By 1900, the prolific revival of styles which characterized the nineteenth century had also generated several distinct reform movements which arose in reaction to an increasingly cluttered historical revival and machine aesthetics. Rococo Revival, the most universally popular style in the United States from the 1840s through the end of the century, and

Renaissance Revival, a style popular since mid-century and dominant in the 1870s, were joined around 1900 by the leaner styles of the Art Nouveau and Arts and Crafts movements.

Above all, the nineteenth century in the United States was a time of industrialization and technological innovation, trends which often ran counter to the contemporary intellectual currents of romanticism and history which dominated the literature and formed the aesthetics and ideals of the century. America's vanguard in the fine and decorative arts reflected the dynamic opposition of these movements, as did the opposing themes of revival and reform in furniture; and styles in furniture, as in clothing, changed from decade to decade throughout the period. While American artisans and designers remained very much under European influence, they continued to adapt each new fashion to the peculiarities of the American marketplace, with the difference

Previous page: *The smoking room of the Rockefeller House, now in the Brooklyn Museum, shows the strong Oriental influence considered correct for this type of room.*
Left: *The so-called Renaissance style as seen in John D Rockefeller's dressing room.*
Below: *Painted designs on black or dark wood were considered Japanese in the 1880s.*

Augustus Eliaers of Boston invented a folding library chair which turned into a step ladder.

that the unique combination of European style elements which gave American furniture its originality in the seventeenth and eighteenth centuries gave way to a new kind of originality after the mid-nineteenth century, when American furniture production entered its most innovative phase. In terms of design, the character of the arts in Victorian America was overwhelmingly popular; and whatever critical assessment may be made, Victorian technology vastly improved the lives of most people, bringing the decorative arts within the reach of the whole population.

By the turn of the century, four principal decorative styles were clearly discernable in the United States. The Beaux Arts style (after the Paris Ecole des Beaux Arts), was – and to a certain extent still is – the dominant mode; Art Nouveau, a continental and particularly French style characterized by stylized, flowing, organic, feminine forms, received only marginal acceptance in practical America, where its influence was largely confined to glasswork and graphics. American Colonial Revival, always a popular theme, had received a tremendous

boost at the 1876 Philadelphia Centennial Exhibition. The newest contender to become a durable American style in the 1900s was Arts and Crafts, which was based on the philosophy and works of England's John Ruskin, William Morris and other reformers who reacted against the negative influences of industrialism on design and society. In America, the unornamented, geometric Arts and Crafts style represented the quest for an artistic yet easily understandable, democratic national style. Just as important if less coherent at this time were the many forms generated by a wave of intense nostalgia for America's pioneer past, and a persistent vogue for collecting antiques of all kinds, which developed in the 1890s, particularly among the wealthy, after the European model and in apparent contempt for all of American nineteenth century design. It is significant that one-half of all the 'antique' furniture in the world today was made in England and France during the first three decades of the twentieth century; every innovative style had to face competition from eclectic revivals, copies and antiques.

Perhaps the overwhelming influence which led to the production of such a wide variety of styles was the enormous increase in the buying public. The population of London multiplied by four in the nineteenth century; the population of New York multiplied by eighty. Hand-in-hand with this sheer increase in size was the growing ascendency of the middle class. The cautious middle-of-the-road values of solidity, practicality, conformism and comfort usurped aristocratic influence over the arts and dominated aesthetic development, leading to an age in which achievement of industrial genius was measured by production and success by profit, as purely artistic considerations took a back seat, and progress and wealth were expressed in abundance of ornament. To the fashion of antique collecting was connected the rising idea of nationalism, expressing itself in

appeared, and the living room made its appearance. Busy bourgeois women had little time for etiquette and formal furniture which was not meant to be sat upon. The introduction of plants and flowers into the living room, the increase of small objects and ornamentation, and the attention to comfort and coziness testify to the movement of the women's influence out of the nursery and the bedroom, to which it had formerly been restricted,

Besides the heavy, ornate furniture popularly associated as 'Victorian,' many surprising and innovative styles also emerged by the end of the nineteenth century. Victorian Americans were obsessed with comfort, but they were equally fascinated with magical health cures, potions, and beneficial devices; the United States made one of its chief contributions to furniture design in the field of innovation – for comfort, health, and multipurpose use. The American public was enthralled with furniture that moved, folded, or converted into other uses as much as with the variety of elaborately embellished Victorian styles. Iron and brass beds, favored for reasons of sanitation and economy of space, reached the peak of their popularity in the last thirty years of the nineteenth century;

Left and below: *Eliaers' Invalid Chair could be folded out to allow the patient to lie down.*

America as an enduring fondness for colonial styles.

The growing emancipation of women, culminating in England and France in suffrage after the First World War, was also a major influence on the appearance of the home. The fashionable attitudes for women in the nineteenth century and the placement of furniture necessary to support these attitudes led to an altering of the very concept of interior space. In the early 1900s the old-fashioned parlor dis-

and the use of metal springs, ratchets, levers, iron bases, revolving supports and convertible furniture was also important in helping Americans make the most use and get the most comfort out of increasingly cramped urban living quarters. The convertible bed was given particular attention in America. Perhaps its apotheosis – and the ultimate expression of nineteenth century middle class pretension – was the bed manufactured by the Paine Furniture Company in the 1880s that folded up into an upright piano which, of course, could not be played. Compact, convertible furniture designed for long distance railroad Pullman cars is legendary for its efficiency. America's interest

in patent furniture may well have originated from the technically brilliant furniture designed for railroad sleeping and dining cars. Similarly designed to save space and labor in the first large-scale offices, American office furniture, in use about 1900, was, like some of the amazing buildings it furnished, way ahead of its time; not until after World War II did mechanized offices appear on the market to forge a link with the past. Although America's romance with mechanized furniture faded quickly after the turn of the century, furniture notable for the modern principles of variability and convertibility had been invented with great creativity to solve many of the new prob-

Below left: *An extravagant rattan chair has a metal device on the legs to allow the sitter to rock.*
Below right: *The nineteenth-century love of ornament is evident in this Hunzinger side chair.*

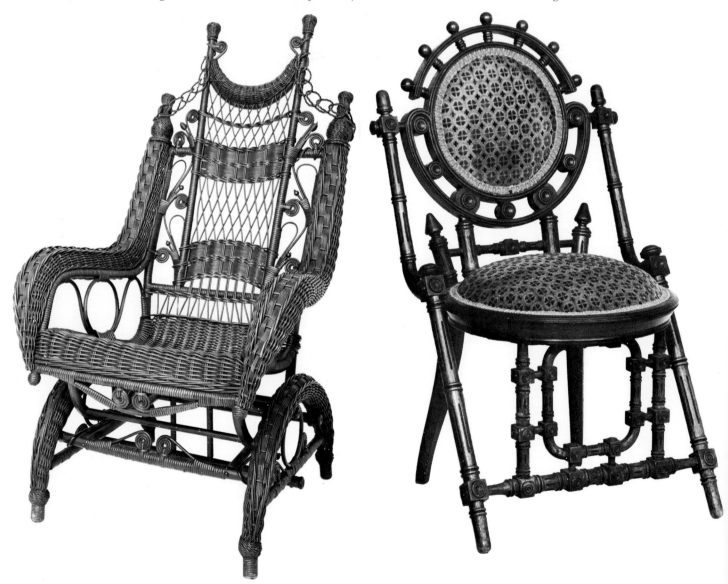

Left: *A highbacked chest of drawers in the Japanese style is covered in woven cane and bamboo ornaments.*
Below: *Wicker work could be used to create chairs of fantastic shape.*

lems that evolved with technological progress; some of the solutions were so new that they in turn influenced social behavior.

Platform rockers and reclining chairs, often with mechanical refinements, were also great late nineteenth century favorites. In 1894, Allan and Brothers of Philadelphia patented their own version of the popular reclining chair, based on the prototype designed by William Watt of England, which incorporated mechanical innovations. Known today as the Morris chair, and nearly as popular then as they are now, the recliners of the age used ratchets or concealed legs to raise and lower their comfortably upholstered backs.

In 1886, a 'fancy chair' fad reached its height. No well-furnished house was without its intriguing fancy chair, which might be a Hunzinger, a high-backed 'English' chair with wings, or an elaborately upholstered Turkish frame chair made up – except for its metal frame and wooden legs – of an extravagant number of coil springs. Towards the end of the century the ever-increasing number of unrelated elements in middle class parlors was complemented by the addition of fancy wicker furniture. Manufactured for virtually every room of the house after 1850, wicker furniture reached the height of its popularity between 1875 and 1910; by the turn of the century, one manufacturer could comfortably claim that no up-to-date house was complete without 'a few pieces of reed and rattan furniture.' The popularity of wicker which, because of its property of ventilation, was also associated with sanitation and health, coincided with some of the trends of the contemporary decorative arts reform movements,

A 'Turkish-style' armchair, so called from the wealth of cords and decorative netting hanging below the overstuffed seat.

as represented by Charles Locke Eastlake's book *Hints on Household Taste*, which advocated 'artistic' furnishings and a return to the hand-made look. But the largest single factor behind wicker's popularity in the late nineteenth century was probably its association with exotic foreign countries; many wicker products or their raw material came from overseas. Exoticism held a fascination as great as comfort for the Victorians, and 'Orientalism' was used loosely to refer to anything exotic and far away, particularly styles from Japan, the Far East, Moorish Spain, and Byzantium. Americans had had ample opportunity to make contact with the Oriental at the many international expositions of the age, especially at the 1876 Centennial Exposition or New Worlds Fair, held in Philadelphia, which reinforced America's fascination with the Japanese decorative arts.

American manufacturers produced large amounts of Japanese-influenced pieces in the last decades of the nineteenth century, some using real bamboo for legs and frames, some using wood worked to look like bamboo; and the Japanese influence – particularly lacquered finishes – was evident in much of the eclectic furniture of the age. In 1882, William H

Vanderbilt had Herter Brothers of New York create a complete 'Japanese Parlour' in his Fifth Avenue mansion. Similarly, the opulent 'Turkish' ('Moorish,' 'Saracenic,' or 'Arab') style was popular throughout the 19th century. During the 1890s, the New York firm of A A Vantine and Company specialized in supplying 'everything that belongs to a genuine Moorish interior.' Many fashionable homes sported a 'Turkish corner' or 'Moorish den,' for smoking or lounging; the popularity of their overstuffed couches and divans reflected the penchant for comfort and relaxed informality which was becoming characteristic of American life. Egyptian forms and symbols also continued to influence American furniture design throughout the nineteenth century (surfacing again briefly in the 1920s), with fashionable cabinet-makers applying Egyptian-inspired ornament to American furniture. An Egyptian revival style, actually a variant of the Renaissance revival, was popular after the Civil War until

Furniture made of hickory with splint seats was popular in the camps of the Adirondack Mountains of New York and in other summer cottages.

the late 1870s; and in 1885, Tiffany and Company of New York was making ormolu and marble mantle sets which represented a popular, romantic version of Egyptian design.

Representing America's growing preoccupation with national identity and its pioneer past, two uniquely American styles of furniture came into their own in the closing years of the nineteenth century. Horn furniture – made from the horns of deer, antelope, moose, buffalo and above all Texas longhorn cattle – evoked the romance of the frontier, especially to consumers in the East, where interest in the American West was highest. Chairs and hatracks were made from the horns of the Texas cattle, and chairs and settees were sometimes upholstered in the skin of the animal from which the horns had come. American Indian and Western motifs often complimented an interior decorating scheme in which such furniture was featured. Borrowing from contemporary technology, a chair made by Wenzel Friedrich from Texas cattle horns in the 1880s and upholstered in jaguar skin, was ingeniously fitted with iron springs for the ultimate in rocking comfort.

Above: *Furniture made from cattlehorns was made for exhibitions, or for those back East who were enthralled by the image of the Old West.*
Below: *Bentwood furniture was popular for its Art Nouveau lines and for its surprising durability.*

Horn veneer used with actual steer horns for an 1880s hatrack.

While today horn furniture is associated with the rough life of the Western frontier, very little of it was of indigenous use; most was made in the fulfillment of romantic fancy for exhibitions, state fairs and sale back East, and not all of it was made in the West. Some of the best was made in Austria and distributed by Tiffany's of New York.

Similar in inspiration were the various forms of rustic furniture often made completely by hand from organic materials and intended for picturesque settings, such as the twisted twig furniture sometimes found among the Oriental and manufactured items in the palatial 'wilderness' camps wealthy New York businessmen built in the Adirondack Mountains in the 1890s. Here, it was imagined, nature lay as unspoiled

as in the Far West; and it was possible to escape urban congestion and enjoy the romantic and renewing presence of nature. While much of this furniture was made by indigenous inhabitants during off-season, of particular note among the rustic styles is Adirondack Hickory, which was made neither in the Adirondacks nor from hickory grown in the Adirondacks, but was manufactured in great quantities between 1898 and 1940 (and in lesser amounts and with more modern materials through the

The Arts and Crafts Movement inspired a return to simpler decoration and less elaborate carving.

1960s) in several factories in Indiana. (Adirondack is a pejorative Indian word meaning 'bark eaters,' used by one tribe to characterize another tribe of supposedly inferior hunting skills.) Characterized by simple functional tables and chairs made from rough-hewn hickory poles with, in many case, the bark still on, and seats and backs woven from the inner bark of the hickory tree, Adirondack Hickory – named for the staggering quantity of hickory furniture imported into the Adirondacks – met the demand for furniture which did not look like it belonged in anything resembling a parlor, and was used to furnish countless cottages, camps and resorts being constructed from Maine to California. Many thousands of tables, settees and chairs, particularly rockers, were produced from Indiana's plentiful hickory trees. The principal features of this self-consciously homespun style were its sturdiness and functionality, and its simplicity gained it the approval of the Arts and Crafts movement. A writer in Gustav Stickley's *Craftsman* magazine, *the* organ for the Arts and Crafts movement in the United States, praised its 'personality and air of definite sincerity.'

The most startling technological furniture of the era, Thonet's bentwood, is still remarkable for its enduring modernity and striking contrast to most Victorian styles. Made exclusively of wood except for small metal parts used at points where the furniture was fastened together, German-born Michael Thonet's bentwood, developed between 1830 and 1857, brought furniture-making from the realm of handicraft into the industrial age, revolutionizing design, production and marketing. His successor built the largest furniture company the world had ever seen.

Thonet's particular innovation was the development of a woodbending process specifically geared to large-scale production of chairs and other furniture. Beginning with steam-bending laminated parts, he came under Prince Metternich's protection, moved to Vienna in 1842, and began experimenting with bending solid wood. In 1855 he perfected the technique of mass-producing solid bentwood furniture from copper beech trees in factories he and his sons designed. In 1859 Thonet brought out his famous Chair No. 14. By 1860, his factory produced 50,000 pieces of furniture a year; in 1876, with production up to 2000 pieces a day, his furniture was introduced to the American

Eastlake's tenets inspired furniture based on a medieval ideal.

public at large at the Centennial Exposition. By 1930, 50 million copies of Chair No. 14 had been produced.

At first the solid beechwood chairs were sold almost exclusively for commercial use in cafes, restaurants and hotels. The opening-up of the United States in the second half of the nineteenth century, together with the development of the colonial countries, provided a huge market for furniture which was cheap, strong, light and easily transportable. Thonet's furniture, available in 1000 styles by the turn of the century, was shipped unassembled or 'knocked-down' in large crates – greatly reducing shipping costs – and assembled with screws at its destination. If it ever began to wobble with use, it could be fixed by tightening the screws.

Even the newly invented ice-box was re-designed according to Eastlake's guidelines.

While the chairs themselves reveal the influence of Rococo Revival styling, Thonet's method of construction reduced the elements of form to its essence; the success of bentwood furniture apparently lies in its simplicity. By the end of the nineteenth century, Thonet's central achievement, Chair No. 14, a bent beechwood chair with a cane seat, was as much at home in fine salons as in middle class drawing rooms, Viennese restaurants, Australian mining towns and American hotels; and Thonet, fulfilling the demands of mass consumption in an exemplary manner, had produced something approaching the 'decorative, noble, popular art' which was reformer William Morris' aspiration.

One of the most widely manufactured and popular fashions of furniture in the last quarter of nineteenth century America was a rectilinear form with spindling, incising and conventionalizing relief carving known as 'Art Furniture' or 'Eastlake,' after the British reformer who inspired it. Charles Locke Eastlake's *Hints on Household Taste*, first published in England in 1868 and in America in 1872, had a profound effect, causing a design revolution on both sides of the Atlantic, particularly among the younger and more intelligent section of the Victorian middle class who had reacted so strongly against the design excesses of the ostentatious French Rococo furniture exhibited at the 1851 Crystal Palace Exhibition in London. Eastlake's book caused a sensation, particularly in America, where it functioned as a consciousness-raiser for a class of consumers for whom ostentation and elaboration had once constituted the only measures of good taste; and it created a demand – particularly in the 1870s and 1880s – for functional, constructively sound, more simply designed furniture.

Charles Lock Eastlake was born to a wealthy Devonshire family in 1836, and named for his uncle Sir Charles Lock Eastlake, a prominent painter who eventually became director of Great Britain's National Gallery. Trained as an architect, a trade he never practiced, Eastlake traveled widely in Europe, was appointed secretary of the Royal Institute of Architecture in 1855 and, capitalizing on his growing reputation as a design critic, wrote *Hints on Household Taste* some ten years later. He was keeper of the National Gallery from 1878-98.

Eastlake was one of many upper class propagandists for aesthetic reform in the England of his day. His writings echoed and amplified the outcry against the excesses of taste produced by waves of revivalism and the increased use of complex technical processes which, while making furniture available to a vastly wider number of people, had inundated design with an abundance of ornament and unsound machine-produced forms. His thesis of simplicity, consistent with the ideas of reform leaders, like Henry Cole, Owen Jones, John Ruskin, William Morris, and Augustus Welby Northmore Pugin, who as early as the 1830s had advocated a return to the indigenous styles and spiritual values of medieval English craftsmanship, found a particularly warm reception among Victorian Americans keen on self-improvement and awed by European arbiters of taste. Eastlake's ideas were moreover quite compatible with the system of production developing in America at the time, and arrived on the shores of an affluent post-Civil War nation eager to establish a new industrial and social order.

Furniture manufacture had begun to blossom in the United States after the Civil War, and by 1870 manufacturing had moved away from the traditional Eastern seaboard centers of New York and Boston to factories in Williamsport, Pennsylvania; Jamestown, New York; Cincinnati, Ohio; Grand Rapids, Michigan; and Chicago, Illinois. By 1890 Chicago led the country in furniture production. Inventions such as Boult's 1874 Carver and Moulder and Blackman's 1875 steam-powered wood-carving machine made possible high-quality factory-made furniture in the Eastlake style; and respected Eastern cabinetmakers, buying suites of furniture from the better factories to resell to their customers in response to demand, placed by implicit craftsman's approval on machine production. By the end of the century 'factory made' was no longer entirely synonymous with poor quality.

Hints on Household Taste was both a lay-philosophic treatise on aesthetics and utility and a breezily practical guide to home furnishings. It offered specific advice on everything from construction and ornamentation to clothing and jewelry. As a theoretical treatise, it promoted the principles of simplicity, functionalism and honesty of construction which were believed to be characteristic of medieval craftsmanship, although Eastlake was careful to stress that it was the 'spirit and principle' of early manufacture he advocated and not any

A decorative easel with gothic motifs was used for displaying and storing artwork in the drawing room or library.

particular style, thus freeing his ideas for application to a wide range of styles in Art Furniture from the modern Gothic to the Oriental. Eastlake particularly disapproved of the shaped or curved forms of Rococo Revival, and stressed solidly constructed simple rectilinear forms which might be accented by the use of turned legs, spindle supports, stylized carving or veneers. He asserted that ornament should be stylized rather than naturalistic, and always related to function. Carved decoration was to be shallow and never inconveniently located, as were the 'knotted lumps' of grapes or roses that often stabbed the sitter in a Rococo chair between the shoulder blades. Varnish was utterly taboo. 'The moment a carved or sculpted surface begins to shine, it loses interest.' Eastlake favored oil-rubbed surfaces and solid strongly-grained woods such as oak, walnut or mahogany, although 'deal' or soft pine was acceptable for inexpensive pieces when painted or stained. Eastlake felt that the machine-carved glued-on ornament commonly found on cheap Renaissance Revival furniture was 'egregiously and utterly bad,' but he did not reject all machine-made furniture. Acknowledging the benefits of mass production, Eastlake maintained that 'Good artistic furniture ought really to be as cheap as that which is ugly.'

Eastlake was principally a critic of taste, not a furniture designer. Actual pieces of furniture designed by him are exceedingly rare. In America, the Eastlake style derived its name from the similarity between furniture manufactured in the 1870s and 1880s and the illustrations in his book, which included such ornamental features as bail handles, brass strap hinges, shallow carving, marquetry, incised or pierced geometric designs, rows of turned spindles, chamfered edges and Gothic-inspired keyhole hardware. Exhibits of 'Modern Gothic' furniture by Kimbel and Cabus of New York and of pieces 'rigidly after the canons of Eastlake' by Mitchell and Rammelsburg of Cincinnati at the 1876 Centennial Exhibition did much to popularize Eastlake's ideas. Modern Gothic, as exemplified by Kimbel and Cabus in ebonized pieces with brass strap hinges, incised geometric designs picked out in gilt and medieval-looking tiles, was popular until about 1885, when the concurrent trend of rectilinear Eastlake furniture ebonized or lacquered and inlaid in the Japanese style, exemplified by furniture produced by Herter

One of the most fashionable furniture makers of the period was Herter Brothers of New York, who designed this chest of ebonized and inlaid cherry.

Brothers of New York, gained the ascendant. Cranes, rushes, butterflies and fans proliferated on furniture of every quality; 'Queen Anne' Reform style featured a profusion of turned elements and spindles.

After the 1876 Exhibition, the Eastlake style was also taken up by manufacturers of cheaper furniture, who until then had not concerned themselves with artistic form. In fact, many who chose to capitalize on the new demand turned out 'East Lake' furniture which had little or nothing to do with Eastlake's principles, causing Eastlake to comment, 'I find American tradesmen continually advertising what they are pleased to call "Eastlake" furniture, with the production of which I have had very little to do, and for the taste of which I should be very sorry to be considered responsible.'

By 1895, Eastlake furniture was no longer

A china closet built at the Craftsmen Workshops has leaded glass doors and hand-hammered copper hardware.

harmoniously to the character of the building in which it was found. His furniture, usually made of oak and solidly constructed, contains modern Gothic and Eastlakian elements, especially in his chairs, which often incorporated turned spindles and bobbins; but his highly individualistic style, sometimes strikingly modern, also contains Queen Anne and American Colonial elements adapted to his interiors, and even on occasion a Byzantine ornament. An armchair designed for the Crane Memorial Library having clean modern lines and discreet turned spindles slyly uses the uprights of the front legs to create the stylized heads of cranes, recalling the library's name.

Richardson's furniture designs were executed by the Boston firm of Irving, Casson, and Davenport. He and his staff looked upon their profession in terms of aesthetic unity – furniture, lighting, windows, and decorative glass were all included in his concern to make his buildings complete and organic works of art. His influence on design reform (he died in 1886)

Armchair by H H Richardson or a member of his staff for the Crane Memorial Library, Quincy, MA.

considered fashionable. But *Hints on Household Taste* had inspired a generation of Americans to be more aware of design principles in their environment; and Eastlake's principles, particularly in America, bridged the gap between William Morris's philosophy of handcrafted furniture, which proved to be affordable only for the affluent few, and the impending expressions of the American Arts and Crafts movement, which were largely mass-produced.

Reaction to Revivalism in the United States was also exemplified in the furniture designed in the 1880s by architect Henry Hobson Richardson. Richardson, who designed numerous public buildings in the Boston area, primarily in the Romanesque style, designed furniture for his and other public buildings according to the premise that furniture, as part of the whole, ought to relate visually and persisted with great effect among a minority of architect-designers in Chicago and the Pacific coast, including Louis H Sullivan and Frank Lloyd Wright.

While Eastlake was the best-known critic of popular taste of the day, William Morris and his Arts and Crafts movement was perhaps the single most important influence on American furniture and design in the decades just before and just after the turn of the century. The philosophical basis for the Arts and Crafts movement began in England in the mid-nineteenth century, following the lead given by Pugin, with the writings of John Ruskin, prolific author and art historian, who saw the Industrial Revolution as a dehumanizing influence responsible for the disintegration of organic social order, and concluded that art and society had been ideally integrated during the

A front fall desk designed and built by Gustav Stickley shows tenon joinery not unlike that of early Southwestern furniture.

early Middle Ages. Ruskin was less concerned with the objects of decorative art than with their effects on their makers. He wholly rejected factory production, believing piece-work in particular was the enemy, asserting that only if each piece of furniture were produced from first to last by the same man could quality of manufacture and the dignity of labor be insured. Ruskin was also the first influential figure to stress the virtues of honesty of expression, integrity of materials, and robust, even crude simplicity in the decorative arts. He advocated antihistoricism and individualism in design.

It remained to William Morris to put Ruskin's theories into practice. A socialist, Morris perceived the shoddiness, ugliness and pretense of a great portion of the English industrial product of the day – which was designed for ease of manufacture and profit rather than beauty or utility – as the inevitable consequence of the

capitalist system, and he believed that the system had reduced the worker to a nonentity totally removed from the conception and design of the articles he helped produce. Morris looked to the medieval model to exemplify his ideal of community and craftsmanship; and in 1861 he formed Morris and Company with several gifted peers, the first in a long line of workshops and communities founded by Morris and other English Arts and Crafts practitioners to combine art and craft in accordance with the ideal of community. Paradoxically, the products of Morris's workshops were luxuries, because his standards were so high; quality goods for the masses at this level was an unattainable goal.

In 1888 a number of English Arts and Crafts societies, including Morris's, formed the Arts and Crafts Exhibition Society to provide a forum for discussion. Almost all of the principal members of the English avant-garde belonged and participated; and as time went on, the Society began to concentrate more and more on just and fitting use of materials, simplicity and functionalism. In the face of demographics, the resistance to machine production also waned. Morris declared, 'We must not liberate ourselves from some material machine or other of steel or brass, but from the huge, immaterial machine of commercial tyranny that oppresses all of our lives.' As the Arts and Crafts movement gained momentum in England, its

Stickley white-oak furniture might be decorated with abstract inlays of metal, especially pewter and copper, and wood.

influence began to be felt on the continent; in 1903, the famous Wiener Werkstaette (Vienna Workshop) was founded in Vienna.

As was the case with Eastlake, Arts and Crafts thinking enjoyed more success in the United States than it ever did on its own home ground. Two men in particular, Gustav Stickley and, to a much lesser extent, Elbert Hubbard, were chiefly responsible for popularizing Arts and Crafts as a decorative style in America.

Elbert Hubbard, unlike Stickley, was not a furniture designer, but a businessman, promoter, folksy philosopher, journalist, and publicist. He first achieved wealth and fame selling soap for his brother-in-law's business in Buffalo. He left the soap business in 1892, traveled, and turned his attention to writing. In 1894, Hubbard visited England and met William Morris at the Kelmscott Press, the private press Morris had founded in 1890 to exemplify Arts and Crafts ideals in printing and binding books. He returned to America and founded the Roycroft Press in East Aurora, New York, after Morris's model, and over the next twenty years (although Hubbard died in 1915

on the *Lusitania*, Roycroft continued producing into the late 1930s) the Roycroft shops expanded under his direction, turning out Arts and Crafts books, furniture, leather goods, china, lamps, bookends, hammered copper trays, pecan patties, Roycroft ties, and apparently anything Hubbard could sell, which was apparently anything. Hubbard, self-styled 'the Fra,' after medieval usage, chose the name Roycroft to honor seventeenth century printers Samuel and Thomas Roycroft; the Roycroft insignia, the orb and cross, was taken from the thirteenth century bookbinder and illuminator Cassidorius. Books remained the primary concern at Roycroft.

The Roycroft cabinetmaking shops were created in 1896 to make furniture for the Roycroft Inn, at which Hubbard lodged the Fords, Rockefellers and other rich and famous guests who came to observe his community. When his distinguished visitors wanted to buy the tables and chairs at the inn, Hubbard realized the

The spindle armchair of white, quarter-sawn oak with a rush seat is a typical example of Stickley design.

potential market for this furniture, and included it in his catalog. Basically a blend of English Arts and Crafts prototypes – the bulbous foot was taken from a design by Arthur Heygate Mackmurdo, copper hardware from a table by Herbert McNair – Roycroft furniture was built by hand with superb joinery from the grades of wood, usually quartersawn oak. Mahogany, ash, walnut and birdseye maple were also used. The furniture often has a reassuringly weighty appearance, and the oak furniture was finished with a dark red-black stain. Although it bears no resemblance to American colonial styles, Hubbard called his furniture 'Aurora Colonial.' He probably intended the mahogany-like stain to insure that his furniture would not be incompatible with the Colonial furnishings which dominated interior decorating at the turn of the century.

The creator of the Roycroft furniture designs is unknown; the designs may have been the work of the individual cabinetmakers – Victor Toothaker, Albert Danner, and Hubert Buffum – who made the pieces after basic, Hubbard-approved guidelines. While much of the furniture is in the best tradition of American Arts and Crafts, the Roycrofters created perhaps more than their share of inept designs, and there is an inconsistency to the craftsmanship and the work as a whole. All the furniture was marked in a prominent place with the orb and cross, or with the word 'Roycroft' incised in Gothic script, often dominating the piece, a tribute to Hubbard's publicist urge. The Roycroft furniture shop employed 80-100 workers at the height of its activity, between 1912 and 1919; the number of pieces produced never approached the volume produced by Stickley and his brothers.

On sale in 1897, Roycroft furniture was among the first Arts and Crafts furniture produced in America, and had a strong influence on this type of design. But the first to make furniture in this style and to use the term 'mission oak' was probably New York furniture manufacturer Joseph P McHugh, who asserted he had designed a variety of pieces in this style in 1884 after being inspired by a chair designed for a church in San Francisco. While his claim does appear to be legitimate, McHugh apparently revised the date by a few years in order to doubly insure his primacy; at any rate, McHugh generated an extraordinary amount of publicity for his mission furniture in trade magazines

and arts periodicals in 1900. But his designs were inept and his construction substandard, and it remained for Gustav Stickley to create the only enduring large body of work in this style.

Shortly after the turn of the century, Gustav Stickley quickly became the principal force behind the Arts and Crafts movement in America. As such he must be considered the single most important figure in the development of new approaches to design in the United States. His 'Craftsman' furniture, a unique synthesis of American Shaker with the Japanese and the medieval, was the first popular modern furniture produced in the United States; and his paradoxical reconciliation of Arts and Crafts with the machine insures his place in history as one of the first machine age designers. Not the least of his accomplishments was *The Craftsman*, the magazine he created and edited between 1901 and 1916, which did more than anything else to propagate the ideas of the

A chest of drawers with tiger maple veneer made at the Craftsman Workshops in 1907.

Arts and Crafts movement throughout America.

Gustav Stickley was born in 1857 in rural Polk County, Wisconsin, the eldest of 11 children. His father was a stone mason and farmer; Gustav and all five of his brothers eventually became furniture manufacturers. Sometime in the 1870s, their father deserted them, and Gustav began making furniture with his uncles and other relatives, eventually becoming a partner in several successful furniture businesses.

In 1898 Stickley visited Siegfried Bing's *Salon de l'Art Nouveau* in Paris, meeting place and showroom for the group of radical designers creating the style known as Art Nouveau. He brought back furniture, glass, jewelry, textiles and metal work from Bing's shop. In the same year he visited England. Morris was dead by that time, but Stickley had ample opportunity to examine first-hand the works of Arthur Heygate Mackmurdo, Charles F A Voysey, Charles Robert Ashbee, Mackay Hugh Baillie Scott, and other leading British Arts and Crafts practitioners. He felt that the British Arts and Crafts philosophy was too exclusive, as he had thought Art Nouveau; but he definitely found the movement 'more in harmony with what I had in mind.' Neither of these European modern styles could fully satisfy the cabinet-maker Stickley; it was difficult for him to accept furniture that was more sculpture and fine art than useful object. But he found William Morris's accomplishments undeniable, and on his return to the United States founded the Gustav Stickley Company in Eastwood, New Jersey, and began experimenting with design.

Stickley originally set out to make a sort of Art Nouveau, but ultimately rejected the style as leading to structurally unsound furniture, and suitable only for decorative purposes. While Shaker, Japanese and medieval elements from his former experience are evident in his work, Stickley's strongest, most direct design influence seems to be English, with a particular debt to architect Baillie Scott, who was closely aligned with Arts and Crafts theory, believed in the importance of the joy to be found in craftsmanship, and rejected machine manufacture and commercialism. Baillie Scott was a proponent of proportion and, above all, of simplicity; and like most of the Arts and Crafts architects of his time, he was also concerned with the total environment, designing furniture for houses which would help create unified interiors. Baillie Scott also designed elaborate formal furniture for clients who could afford it. While Stickley demonstrably adapted some of the better design elements from his work – a side chair stretcher here, an apron there – his Craftsman furniture remained democratically unornamented. As much as he owes to English and continental designers, his furniture is consistently truer to basic Arts and Crafts philosophy than any body of work by any other designer.

A slat-back Colonial-revival side chair designed by Wallace Nutting overemphasizes some of the features of the furniture of early New England.

An oak, spindle child's bed designed by Stickley bears all familiar details of construction.

Stickley's straight-lined, well-made, hand-finished and intentionally and unusually heavy furniture, which he called 'Craftsman,' was meant to be set in place and left there. A few pieces featured minimal inlaid decoration, but Craftsman furniture as a whole was free of any applied decoration; Stickley believed ornamentation must be functional. Structural features became the focal point of ornamentation, as in the frequently exposed mortise and tenon joints, sometimes keyed for strength, and in the exposed dowels used for accent. Hand-wrought and carefully finished iron or copper hardware was given the same meticulous attention as the wood. Solid American white oak, quartersawn to add strength and to expose the wood's decorative medullary rays, was preferred. The basic ornament was the wood itself, which was not stained but 'fumed' (ammonia fumes reacting with the tannic acid in the oak produced the characteristic rich nut-brown color), and finished with a mixture of one-third white shellac and two-thirds German lacquer. The furniture was then waxed. Plain dark leather was used for upholstery; and library tables might be covered with leather and fastened around the edges with iron or copper brads. Stickley described his furniture as 'constructed on primitive lines, planned for comfort, durability, and beauty, expressing the true spirit of democracy.' A chair was to look like what it was. 'The piece is . . . first, last and all the time a *chair*, and not an imitation of a throne, not an exhibit of snakes and dragons in a wild riot of misapplied wood-carving.'

Each piece of Craftsman furniture was marked with Stickley's motto *Als Ik Kan* – 'As I Can' – adapted from Jan van Eyck after William Morris's *Si je puis*. Much of the work was done by hand by workmen with whom Stickley, even

Leather seats trimmed with brass nails and hand-hammered hardware are typical accents on Stickley furniture.

after the era of profit-sharing, maintained unusually warm relations. But Stickley was also one of the first to recognize the true value of the machine, used as a craftsman's tool, to accomplish certain basic and repetitive tasks, and to save the craftsman time and energy for more important considerations. He rejected the use of machinery to simulate hand carving in imitation of period furniture, working with the machine to create an increasingly lean style which grew naturally from its strengths. As much as his love of wood, fine craftsmanship and quality construction tie him to nineteenth century Arts and Crafts design reform, his belief in functionalism and pure form and his enlightened use of technology prefigure the International Style and mark him as an innovator in modern twentieth-century design.

In 1900, Stickley first showed his new Craftsman designs at the Furniture Exposition in Grand Rapids; in 1901 he changed the name of his company to United Crafts, a profit-sharing cooperative of decorative arts modeled after the medieval crafts guild, and clearly reflecting the principles of William Morris. Until 1915, when bankruptcy forced him out of business, Stickley continued designing and refining Arts and Crafts furniture. As his designs approached great functionalism and purer form, his business also changed enormously. In 1905, with the main elements of his style in place and commercial success mushrooming, Stickley dropped the idea of profit-sharing, expanded, and changed the name of his operations to Craftsman Workshops. Most of the staggering amount of furniture that he produced was manufactured between 1904 and 1910, with 1909 generally acknowledged as the heyday of the Craftsman fashion. His workshops operated six days a week, and his catalogs averaged about 150 designs; the 1909 catalog listed Morris Chairs, bookcases, library tables, dining- room tables and chairs, china cabinets, sideboards, bedroom furniture and 18 different rockers, including a child's model. Stickley made a rocking version of almost every chair he produced. In 1905 he moved his executive offices and editorial offices for *The Craftsman* from Eastwood to Manhattan; and in 1913 his various enterprises were housed in the twelve-story Craftsman building, the center of an empire that stretched across the United States with over 50 representatives in major cities.

Stickley's furniture was aggressively imitated and mass-produced. At the height of Arts and Crafts popularity it was copied by Sears Roebuck, Come-Packt, Macy, Gunn, Limberts Arts and Crafts (Grand Rapids), Retting, Hawthorne, Life Time and many others. Stickley's brothers, who at one time or another were all in business with him, manufactured their own copies. Leopold and Julius George (L & JG) were Gustav's most successful imitators. Charles had his own factory, and George and Albert manufactured under the names 'Stickley Brothers' and 'Quaint Furniture.' None of these imitators approached the quality of Gustav's furniture, but some had better business sense, and their cheaply made pieces sold well. After Stickley's bankruptcy, Leopold Stickley bought the old Craftsman factory from Gustav in 1918; the L & JG Stickley Company, Inc, still manufactures colonial reproduction Cherry Valley Furniture in Fayetteville, New York.

Building on his early success with Craftsman furniture, Stickley had rapidly extended his activities into all areas of the decorative arts. Following trips to Europe and Asia in 1902-3, he formed a textile department. Eventually one floor of the Craftsman building was devoted to rugs and interior decorating, and another to draperies and house furnishings. Metal work, rugs, lighting fixtures, silver, copper, brass and many other items were released with the Craftsman label. Stickley also styled himself an architect. By 1902 he was publishing house designs in *The Craftsman*, and by 1912 he was building Craftsman houses, examples of which can still be found in many of the 'Garden Cities' which were popular before World War I. He designed Craftsman gardens and Craftsman landscapes to complement Craftsman houses. In 1908, Stickley bought the 600-acre Craftsman Farms in New Jersey, upon which he erected model

L and JG Stickley also designed furniture, but this spring seat sofa proves that their designs were less original than Gustav's.

structures. Food grown on Craftsman Farms was served on Craftsman place settings by Japanese waiters in the Craftsman Restaurant atop the Craftsman building. The Farms were also the projected site for a model pedagogic enterprise. Stickley clearly over-extended himself, and later allowed that he thought bad business practices had ruined him. But the bankruptcy of The Craftsman, Inc, on 24 March 1915, was also rooted in the collapse of the entire Arts and Crafts movement, and in the change in perspective which came with World War I. German associations with pre-war modern architecture and decorative arts devalued all aspects of modern design. By 1920, Americans, now citizens of one of the world's great powers,

had embraced Colonial reproductions in a frenzy of national identity and xenophobia.

A major contributing factor during the years of Stickley's phenomenal success was *The Craftsman* magazine, which functioned both as a promotional arm and as the essential organ of information for the Arts and Crafts movement in America and elsewhere. In *The Craftsman* Stickley first published pictures of his Craftsman furniture, and elaborated its aesthetic and philosophical virtues. During the magazine's 16 years of production, Stickley, his staff, and guest writers contributed poems, plays and articles covering every aspect of culture and the Arts and Crafts movement. It published a total of 221 working plans for Craftsman house do-it-yourself projects and plans for the amateur furniture builder were also an important feature. This history and content of *The Craftsman* fairly charts the course of the Arts and Crafts movement in America; and its effect on molding American taste may be Stickley's most enduring achievement. When *The Craftsman* ceased publication with the December 1916 issue, the Arts and Crafts movement was to all intents and purposes finished.

Far left: *Mahogany clock designed by George Elmslie.*
Left: *An oak rocker designed by Charles Rohlfs.*

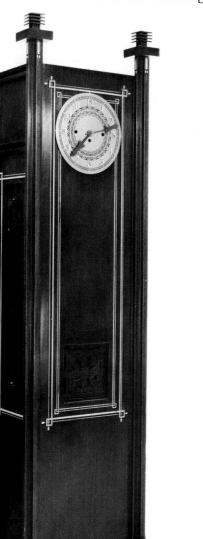

The term 'mission oak', commonly applied to Craftsman and Roycroft furniture and to Arts and Crafts furniture produced in the same style, appears to have arisen out of a mixture of honest confusion and commercial exploitation. Neither Hubbard nor Stickley, its foremost exponents, particularly favored this designation, but both Hubbard and L & JG Stickley eventually acknowledged its popularity by using it in their catalogs. As used by the manufacturers, 'mission' was meant to imply that Arts and Crafts furniture was in the historical style of the furniture made and used in the Spanish missions of the old Southwest. This was emphatically not the case, but the name caught on, riding on the wave of nostalgia for the American past and the Old West. The issue was further complicated because Stickley was fond of saying in his literature that his furniture was designed to fulfill its 'mission of usefulness.' Similar statements in his writings about his furniture's 'mission' compounded the confusion. In a 1904 newspaper interview Stickley acknowledged a philosophical kinship between his furniture and the plain functional styles of the California missions, but denied

Left: *An Art Nouveau card table.*
Middle: *Oak chair designed by Louis Comfort Tiffany.*
Right: *Tall-backed chair designed by Charles Rohlfs typifies the verve of Art Nouveau.*

that his styles were in any way derived or copied from them. There is no reason to doubt his assertion; Stickley considered his furniture 'a revolution against the historical style.'

Throughout the era of Eastlake's consciousness-raising and Stickley's self-conscious style, most Americans continued to buy reproductions and 'factory' furniture of all kinds. It would be a mistake to believe that most Americans had the education, sophistication or the means to keep up with fashions in furniture. Manifestly, Stickley's dream of creating a durable national style failed; the fall 1909 Sears & Roebuck catalog featured, at the peak of the mission fashion, an 'Extra Large Massive Selected Quarter Sawed Solid Oak Beautifully Carved Rocker,' a vaguely colonial rocker in golden oak with spindling, applied ornament, and 'carving' that would have set Eastlake's teeth on edge. All the furniture advertised was

A linen or shirtwaist chest designed by Stickley in 1905 is reminiscent of the early New England chests.

During the second decade of the twentieth century, patent furniture – as exemplified by the in-a-door bed, the davenport bed, and the evolution of the Morris Chair, now with a push-button to make a foot stool pop out from underneath – again commanded serious attention from the American public. 'Borax' furniture – cheap, showy furniture particularly intended for the installment trade – continued high in popularity. This colloquial use of 'borax' is attributable to the premiums given with a popular cleaning compound of the day, or to corrupt foreign language slang, or possibly to the fact that borax was used in the manufacture

An American curio cabinet imitates the French Art Nouveau style even to the popular poppy carvings.

in golden oak or golden oak finish, popular America's favorite color since the 1870s and 1880s, when all factory 'Gothic' and 'medieval' was in black walnut; within another decade, the dark colors would return to fashion.

By the turn of the century, for the majority of Americans the reproduction era was in full flower. Rooms at the 1876 Centennial Exhibition celebrating America's colonial heritage had helped usher in a colonial revival, and mass-produced colonial curiosities poured off the Midwestern furniture factory assembly lines, vying with equally mass-produced renditions of 'Beaux Arts Revival,' wicker, Queen Anne, patent, Japanese or Oriental, Tudor, and 'Quaint' furniture, quaintness being a label sanctioning the manufacture of reproduction furniture only remotely resembling the original. However, quality reproduction in the spirit of Arts and Crafts honesty of construction also appeared, and recognition of American furniture as worthy of serious study culminated in the Hudson Fulton Exhibition of 1909 in the Metropolitan Museum of Art in New York. By World War I, Colonial revival completely suffocated taste for the simple lines of mission oak, which itself had already greatly dampened enthusiasm for the curves of Art Nouveau. Before going under completely – he died in obscurity in 1942 – even Stickley abandoned Arts and Crafts and designed a line of colonial furniture he called 'Chromewald.'

of certain enamels – enamel furniture in white, ivory and gray made a comeback and became something of a craze at the time. In 1917, when America entered the war, furniture styles other than borax were neglected, although throughout the postwar years the furniture industry boomed along with the housing industry. One result of a Florida real estate boom was 'Spanish' furniture: any piece of furniture with an arcade of turned spindles was termed 'Spanish.' The style was produced at a furious rate. A similar style from California was 'Monterey,' a sort of glorified Mission.

While in England the Arts and Crafts movement strove toward simple, strong forms without completely divesting furniture of historical influences, on the continent reaction to the over-ornamental historical forms and the ugliness of the industrial world took the form of an attempt to create a universe of design totally

An oak dropfront desk designed by Rohlfs uses pierced wood, carvings and hammered brass hardware for decoration.

An ebonized oak hall bench designed by Rohlfs.

independent of all traditional styles. Between 1890 and 1910, the movement called Art Nouveau developed in Europe; roots again are partly traceable to mid-nineteenth century England and Ruskin and Morris's innovation of natural forms for decorative purposes, but 'Art Nouveau' remains an elusive term. Historically, it originated with Siegfried Bing's Paris shop *L'Art Nouveau*, opened in 1896, which specialized in unique, artistic furnishing and artworks in the modern style. But Art Nouveau was more a philosophy than an identifiable, unified turn of the century decorative arts style, and it is best understood both as a generic expression of a widespread renewal of artistic ideas in Europe, and as a specifically French and Belgian style of decorative design characterized by sensual, flowing, naturalistic and stylized organic forms.

The American public did not become aware of Art Nouveau until the height of its development, when visitors to the Paris *Exposition Universelle* in 1900 discovered the decorative Art Nouveau lamps, railings and entrances to the Metro, and visited Bing's *Maison de L'Art Nouveau* at the exposition. Press coverage of the exposition generated a wave of interest in the new art, photographs appeared in American magazines and manufacturers, sensing a new market, rose to the occasion. Unlike their Viennese and Scottish counterparts, however, American manufacturers were very much out-

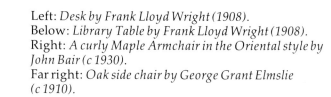

Left: *Desk by Frank Lloyd Wright (1908).*
Below: *Library Table by Frank Lloyd Wright (1908).*
Right: *A curly Maple Armchair in the Oriental style by John Bair (c 1930).*
Far right: *Oak side chair by George Grant Elmslie (c 1910).*

siders to this style, and never succeeded in creating a successful and distinctive American variant. American Art Nouveau furniture was for the most part a mass-manufactured commercial product attempting to capitalize on the sudden popularity of a new style; but Art Nouveau was by its very nature not easily adapted to the machine or to large-scale production. In France, the best Art Nouveau pieces were expensive handmade works of art, each unique.

American designers attempted to standardize Art Nouveau motifs into a simple vocabulary the public could easily understand and identify with – women with flowing hair and clinging garments, tulips, lilies and twisting, stem-like lines already recognizable from contemporary graphic styles. Standardizing Art Nouveau structural forms proved even more difficult, and for the most part Art Nouveau decoration was grafted onto forms reflecting the popular revival styles of the day; Art Nouveau marquetry, carving, fabric and finish found its way onto heavy golden oak, mahogany or walnut sofas of 1890s reproduction styles.

Although French Art Nouveau often employed carving and marquetry together, in America two distinct categories of furniture

emerged. One, as exemplified by S Karpen Brothers and The Tobey Company, both of Chicago, employed only carving, although never deeply enough to define a structural element, as was often the case on the continent. The other employed only marquetry, but because the inlay was usually purchased ready-made, it was sometimes unrelated to the piece on which it appeared; imported marquetry still causes some confusion as to the origin of the pieces.

As a movement, Art Nouveau in America became a style of ornamentation, essentially limited to areas other than furniture. Relatively few pieces of furniture were made, and the style enjoyed only a brief vogue before succumbing to the broader middle-class demand for mission furniture. Artus Van Briggle's Lorelei vase, Will H Bradley's posters, and above all Louis Comfort Tiffany's glass and glass lampshades received international acclaim, but American Art Nouveau furniture was rarely constructed with the same flowing forms and curvilinear outline so popular in Europe, and cannot compare with the handcrafted, often one-of-a-kind Art Nouveau furniture of Belgium and France. With its aura of Old World decadence and sensuality, Art Nouveau could not compete with turn-of-the-century America's nostalgia for her pioneer

By 1898, Rohlfs was creating oak Art Nouveau side chairs which were considerably closer to their European counterparts than any mass-produced American Art Nouveau products. Rohlfs undoubtedly received more attention outside the United States than any other American designer of the era. His collection of furniture exhibited at Turin in 1902 was very well received by European and English critics. Rohlfs was elected a member of the Royal Society of Arts in London, and was commissioned to provide furniture for Buckingham Palace.

Will H Bradley was one of the few American designers who attempted to reconcile the mission, Arts and Crafts and Art Nouveau styles. 'The American Beardsley' also set out to create a definite style of his own; his furniture and room interior designs commissioned for *The Ladies Home Journal* in 1901 and 1902 display rectilinear furniture that is severe and rigid, structural and functional, with all the Arts and Crafts features of tenon and key, diamond-shaped windows and built-in furniture; but the non-structural areas of his furniture and wall space are gaily decorated with painted curvilinear designs, cut-outs, elaborate metal hinges and inlaid metal panels.

Bradley, like Stickley, also used 'mission' when he meant 'function': 'Printed matter does not fulfill its mission unless it answers to the broadest interpretation of the word "appropriate".' Bradley felt his mission was 'to inject imagination, taste (art) into the cheap and commonplace. Because it is ... democratic [and] widely distributed does not mean that it has to be ugly.' Significantly, his furniture designs, no pieces of which are known to exist, prefigure in their severity of line the transition to a machine aesthetics which was to be more fully explored by later generations. The movement of his style away from the curvilinear to the rectilinear likewise charts the failure of Art Nouveau to establish itself as ornament in America.

The modern era can be defined as the acceptance of the machine as a positive and creative aesthetic force. For the United States, particularly after the decline of Arts and Crafts, much of the impetus for the new forms which were to emerge came from the Midwest, particularly Chicago, where one of the most significant architectural movements of the twentieth century – the so-called Prairie School – also led to the production of some precedent-setting furniture.

past and quest for national myth; and mission furniture, with its connotations of the clean, the healthy, the sturdy, the simple and the honest, carried the day. Significantly, America's best-known designers, the Greene Brothers and Frank Lloyd Wright, architects who addressed the total environment and designed handcrafted furniture, did not choose to work in the continental idiom, apparently rejecting the ornate organic French styles in favor of the plainer forms more acceptable to their countrymen.

One American designer who did utilize the curvilinear French idiom to create handcrafted one-of-a-kind pieces was Charles Rohlfs of Buffalo. At first Rohlfs' work was simple and functional, and of very high quality; but unlike other Arts and Crafts designers, Rohlfs decorated the rectilinear outlines of his oak furniture with delicate carving and marquetry, in a style that may have been suggested by the exterior decoration of Chicago architect Louis Sullivan.

Right: *Chair designed for Imperial Hotel in Tokyo, by Frank Lloyd Wright.*
Far right: *Two inlaid sidechairs and a mahogany vitrine designed by Charles and Henry Greene circa 1907.*
Far right below: *The H H Richardson bedroom in the Glessner House in Chicago combines several periods of nineteenth-century furniture into an agreeable whole.*
Below right: *Designed in 1904, this Frank Lloyd Wright chair is made of painted steel and oak. It predates the bent-tubular chairs of Breuer by over twenty years.*
Below: *Rocking chairs with elongated back, designed by Charles Rohlfs in 1901.*

A walnut inlay bookcase design by Isaac Scott copies a design from Eastlake's Hints on Household Taste.

After the Civil War, Chicago developed rapidly as a design and manufacturing center. By 1875, master designer-craftsman Isaac Scott, who came to Chicago from Philadelphia, was designing exemplary Eastlake-inspired furniture; the famous inlaid walnut bookcase of eclectic medieval design with its cornice panel of birds, leaves and flowers, which he designed for John J Glessner, is a masterpiece of modern Gothic, comparable to the best furniture being produced in the East. Chicago continued to more than keep pace with the evolution of design reform in America. In 1897 the Chicago Arts and Crafts Society was formed, and in 1903 the William Morris Society of Chicago was founded. The style and quality of the Prairie School also crystalized in the early 1890s through the teachings and works of Architects Louis H Sullivan and J S Silsbee, whose students and young employees included Frank Lloyd Wright and George Grant Elmslie. Sullivan's use of bold, stylized ornament as an integral part of his buildings was to have a profound effect on the young designers who worked in his office. Elmslie, a Scot who emigrated to America, joined Sullivan's firm (Adler & Sullivan) in 1889, becoming chief designer in 1895. The furniture he designed for his more important buildings, usually in oak, was less rectilinear and geometric than Wright's, with ornament that was more organic and closer in style to that of Sullivan. In 1907 he designed the Henry B Babson house, as well as simple oak furniture to furnish it; five years later he designed a group of mahogany furniture for Babson, including the famous mahogany grandfather clock case now in the Art Institute of Chicago.

Frank Lloyd Wright, whose architecture, furniture, and writings in architectural theory have earned him a place as one of the greatest pioneers in modern design, worked for a time in the office of J S Silsbee, becoming chief draftsman for Adler & Sullivan in 1888. The characteristic which links his furniture with that of Elmslie, George Washington Maher, and others of the Chicago School is the conception of the building and its interior as 'proceeding from main motifs to minor motifs, interrelating and to the last terminal all of a piece.' In this he reflects the influence of Richardson. In 1908 Wright wrote, 'The most truly satisfactory apartments are those in which most or all of the furniture is built in as a part of the original scheme. The whole must always be considered as an integral unit . . . A building should appear to grow easily from its site and be shaped to harmonize with its surroundings.' The furniture should extend and reflect the lines of the building, emphasizing its essential features. Wright's concept of the structural importance of the furniture in relation to the whole is also grounded in his love of Japanese design. Like many Americans, Wright was impressed by the open design of the typical Japanese building exhibited at the 1893 Chicago Columbian Exhibition; he visited Japan in 1905. The Prairie houses he designed in the first decade of the twentieth century feature an adaptation of this open floor plan, and set the stage for an era of American suburban houses yet to come.

Wright also felt that furniture should be designed 'in simple shapes for the machine . . . straight lines and rectangular forms.' For above all, 'The machine is the normal tool of our civilization; give it work that it can do well; nothing is of greater importance.' Addressing the Chicago Arts and Crafts Society in 1901, in a lecture entitled 'The Art and Craft of the Machine,' Wright declared, 'The machine has liberated the beauties of nature in wood ... Is this not ... precisely the process of omission which Morris championed?' Wright extolled 'The clean cut straight-line forms that the machine can render far better than would be possible by hand. Bring out the nature of the materials, let this nature intimately into your scheme'.

Frank Lloyd Wright's furniture must be regarded as architectural sculpture rather than merely utilitarian objects. Although he rejected the Arts and Crafts movement for its backward inability to understand the machine, he was firmly rooted in the movement, and not only from his preceptors. Wright met Charles Robert Ashbee, one of the most important figures in the English Arts and Crafts movement, in Chicago in 1900, and visited the Ashbees in England. Ashbee eventually wrote the preface to the second edition of Wright's work, which was responsible for making Wright known in Europe. In his preface Ashbee delineated the connection between his and Wright's ideas and the ideas of Walter Gropius, founder of the Bauhaus, and thus established the link between the English Arts and Crafts movement and the European movement toward functional design.

Wright's furniture designs rapidly moved away from the fluid organic ornament of Sul-livan to a strictly geometric functional style based on rectangles, slats and flat surfaces. As much as he professed to detest mission furniture, the square-shaped oak furniture he designed for his famous Robie house in 1908 appears to be mission-inspired. Chairs he designed in 1895 are likewise often indistinguishable from mission; his furniture seems actually to have anticipated the square Craftsman-style furniture which was to follow. An armchair in pine produced in 1904 has bottom stretchers which extend through the legs, a method of construction also used by Gustav Stickley; a dark-stained oak chair designed the same year, as if to demonstrate the versatility of his repertoire, shows how strongly he was influenced by the Japanese. Some of the most striking of Wright's furniture displays an unprecedented open geometricity – perhaps owing something to Japanese architecture – as exemplified in an oak library table designed for the Ray W Evans house in 1908.

Wright's faith in the machine and in the adaptive use of materials enabled him to become one of the few designers who was not swept away in the cultural upheaval of World War I, and whose work more than kept pace with a new middle class of technicians and

Charles and Henry Greene designed this circular dining room table in 1908.

working professionals to whom neither Arts and Crafts nor Art Nouveau supplied design or social answers. Especially during the years 1914-1916, when the extreme *De Stijl* group, stressing shapes natural to the machine and its products, was taken with his concepts, Wright's influence was international; the dawn of the modern furniture movement is synonynmous with the rise of Wright's international reputation.

On the West Coast, the Greene brothers, Charles Sumner and Henry Mather, whose architecture is reminiscent of Wright's, designed furniture which gained them an international reputation. Born in Cincinnati, the Greene brothers studied architecture at MIT,

and moved to Pasadena in 1893. Adding to their interest in Japanese and Spanish Mission architecture, Charles visited Europe in 1901, where he was taken with aspects of Swiss chalet architecture and English Arts and Crafts styles. Between 1907 and 1909, the brothers supplied four of the houses they designed in and around Pasadena with elegant furniture, usually in walnut or teak, and inlaid with ebony, fruitwood, and semi-precious stones. Charles Robert Ashbee, who visited California in 1909, had this to say of their furniture: 'I think C Sumner Greene's work beautiful; among the best there is in this country. Like Lloyd Wright, the spell of Japan is upon him, he feels the beauty and makes magic out of the horizontal

The dining room of the Gamble House in Pasadena, by the Greene brothers, has a strong Japanese influence.

design reformers, the ornate Victorian clutter of the 1890s began to open up, and the stage was set for the emergence of new forms.

After the brief sputter of Art Nouveau and the decline of Arts and Crafts, America remained impervious to the stirring of the new styles in Europe, and as the twentieth century progressed, American furniture settled into an era almost exclusively directed toward antiques or colonial reproductions. The designs of Frank Lloyd Wright received little encouragement, perhaps because his thought processes outstripped current social and industrial reality, and American design as a whole remained untouched by the continental revolutions of the *De Stijl* group and the Bauhaus and by such trend-setting cultural events as the pre-war Ballets Russes productions of *Schéhérézade* and *Thamar*, which affected not only dress and decoration on the continent and in England, but had a powerful influence on seat-furniture and manners, persisting into the 1920s.

The 1925 International Exposition of Decorative Arts (*Exposition Internationale des Arts Decoratifs et Industriels Modernes*) in Paris brought together many of the divergent currents of both pre- and post-war European design. Source of the term 'Art Deco,' the exposition had originally been scheduled for 1915, but postponed on account of the war; and America, with neither modern decorative art nor any significant movement in that direction, did not participate. Advanced American design at the time was confined to architecture, usually to skyscrapers intended for commercial use.

But if Americans went to the exposition empty-handed, they came back carrying everything they saw; the impact of the exposition on the United States was earth-shaking. The country, booming economically after the war and refreshed by wartime European contacts, was enthralled by the new shapes and use of new materials. By the late 1920s, major department stores in the United States were staging their own exhibitions, and by the end of the decade decorators were casually borrowing ideas and motifs from industry. Household furnishings, reflecting modern technology, at last showed signs of moving with the spirit of the age; but it remained to the following decades to establish the new styles in America.

line, but there is in his work more tenderness, more subtlety, more self-effacement than in Wright's work. It is more refined and has more repose.'

Despite the incredible amount of thought and energy that went into furniture in America during the nineteenth century, neither Gustav Stickley nor any of the other reformers succeeded in their mission of producing an enduring style of furniture, national or otherwise, and no new styles persisted for more than a few years into the twentieth century. The most important contribution of this era must be seen as the raising of furniture and the decorative arts to a level of consideration more on a par with the fine arts. Largely through the efforts of

6
The Modern Period:
American Furniture Since 1929

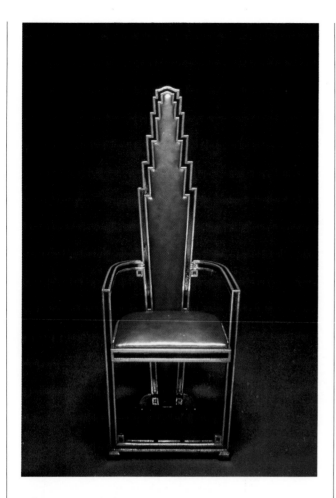

Above: *An armchair designed by Abel Faidy is reminiscent of Art Deco architecture.*
Below: *A dining room table by Faidy (1927) has the strong verticals and angles that mark the piece as Art Deco.*
Previous page: *The Main Lobby of Radio City Music Hall typifies the Art Deco Style in the United States.*

Although the stock market crash would eventually plunge the nation into the Great Depression, expansiveness set the keynote in the decade after World War I. Artists and the public alike were captivated by visions of a future in which the machine would unleash undreamed of possibilities. The liberation that machines promised to bring to society had distinctly democratic overtones. Through mass production techniques, well-designed furniture could be enjoyed by the masses.

The United States, long Europe's stepchild in matters of culture, was ready to discard its dependence on reproductions and assume a role of equality, if not yet leadership, in furniture design. The growing confidence Americans were acquiring in matters of taste was coupled in the case of furniture with the deep affinity for the pragmatic and egalitarian elements of a medium which combined craftsmanship and functional value with art.

Society's increasing mobility was having a profound impact on how people lived. Ultimately this would mean changes in how the houses were decorated and a re-examination of the very purpose of furniture. More immediately, it meant Americans were on the go – by car, train, ship and airplane. In these affluent times, Europe was a mecca for artists, the rich and trendsetters, and when Americans traveled abroad, they brought back the latest cultural currents. And of even more important and long-lasting influence were the architects and furniture-makers who joined the waves of immigrants. Austrian architect Joseph Urban emigrated in 1911 and designed the interiors for the Boston and Metropolitan Opera Houses. Raymond Loewy, born in Paris, came to the United States in 1919. Finnish architect Eliel Saarinen, after a visiting professorship term at the University of Michigan in 1924, stayed on to head the newly founded Cranbrook Academy of Art, which was soon to play an important role in furniture design.

The major furniture event in Europe had been the 1925 Paris *Exposition des Arts Decoratifs et Industriels Modernes*, which launched Art Deco. Reflecting a schism that affected American furniture design for the rest of the modern period, German designers were not invited until too late to attend. Herbert Hoover, then Secretary of Commerce, had declined to send an American entry to the Exposition on the grounds that the United States had no modern

design. He did, however, appoint a commission to attend and prepare a report for American manufacturers.

Art Deco capitalized on luxurious ornament, lush textures and rich color. It went by many names: Jazz Modern, Zigzag, Style 1929, Twenties Style. Neoclassical in spirit, it emphasized stylized floral patterns and bold geometrics, inspired by the contemporary interests in pre-Columbian artifacts, Ancient Egypt and trends on stage and film. The characteristic stepped-back look of Art Deco architecture was imitated briefly in furniture. Its finest executions may have been the Radio City Music Hall in New York. There Minnesotan Donald Deskey used chrome, Bakelite and aluminum, along with neon lights, to create an appropriately dramatic and stylized decor with waterfall, zodiac and Mayan motifs.

Left: *Heavy pewter inlay in a side chair of ebonized wood mark a turn to the use of metal in furniture.*
Below: *The use of new materials such as Bakelite and Chrome, as well as tall mirrored surfaces and large murals, found in the downstairs lounge of Radio City Music Hall.*

Left: *A Man's Den designed by Joseph Urban for the Special Exhibition, The Architect and the Industrial Arts, in 1929.*
Below: *A Woman's Bedroom from the same exhibition.*

The style of the Paris exposition made its way into popular American taste with the help from New York department stores B Altman and Lord & Taylor, which organized an exhibit of modern French furniture under the supervision of architect Ely Jacque Kahn. Macy's held its own 'Art in Trade Exposition' with rooms by the Austrian Josef Hoffmann, the German Bruno Paul and New York furniture designers Eugene Schoen and Kem Weber. New industrial materials like Formica and black, glass-like Vitrolite began to make their appearance in the new furniture.

If any event launched the modern age in America, however, it was the 1929 'The Architect and the Industrial Arts' exhibit at the Metropolitan Museum of Art in New York. Richard Bach, a curator of industrial arts for the Metropolitan who had served as one of Hoover's commissioners for the Paris exposition, organized the exhibition. Since there was still so little American furniture in the new style, it had to be designed by architects: Joseph Urban, Eugene Schoen, Raymond Hood, Ralph T Walker and Eliel Saarinen.

Included in the Metropolitan exhibition were a circular table with geometric inlays and fluted side chairs which Saarinen had designed for the dining room of his house at Cranbrook. The exhibition was scheduled to run for six weeks. but the first Sunday after it opened, 10,000 people came, and the exhibit was extended to six months.

Below: *Marcel Breuer's Wassily chair was the first bent-tubular-steel chair of importance. It is still made today.*

Below: *The dining room furniture designed by Eliel Saarinen uses various woods and inlays.*
Right: *Apartment House Loggia designed by Raymond M Hunt for the Special Exhibition.*

While German furniture designers had been preempted from the 1925 Paris exposition, in America their impact was felt at the 1929 Metropolitan exhibition. The German art school known as the Bauhaus had, since 1919, been promoting the idea that the artists must first be craftsmen. Students and faculty studied the machine and its implications for design. The Bauhaus interest in geometric forms had drawn its inspiration from the group of Dutch artists known as *De Stijl* but the Bauhaus was more concerned with matters of function. Marcel Breuer's famous Wassily chair of tubular steel and leather had been introduced in 1925, followed by Ludwig Mies van der Rohe's cantilevered tube chair. While Bauhaus furniture was dependent on craftsmanship rather than mass production, its reliance on basic geometric shapes, consciously imitating machines, gave the appearance of industrial production.

If the Metropolitan's exhibition launched modern furniture in the United States, it represents but one event that marked the explosion of interest in the 'modern' and laid the groundwork for future currents in furniture design. At the Barcelona International Exposition of 1929, Mies van der Rohe, who succeeded Gropius as director of the Bauhaus, designed

Below: *Chair designed by Hammon Kroll uses simple lines and no external decoration.*

the glass and marble German Pavilion and introduced his Barcelona chair. Considered one of the quintessential chairs of the twentieth century because of the eloquent simplicity of its curved metal legs and tufted leather cushions, the Barcelona chair exemplified the 'less is more' philosophy. The next year, 1930, found Mies van der Rohe at the Stockholm Exhibition alongside Gropius and French architect Le-Corbusier in what reflects the cross-fertilization process that began between the wars and resumed in the 1940s. The Scandinavians were to provide an important countercurrent to the Bauhaus designers, who so vehemently argued for a break with tradition.

Although the Depression put a damper on the movement to create new furniture for a new age, it was clear it could do no more than slow it down. The American furniture industry had reached its largest production capacity by 1929. In 1928, *Collier*'s described the new look as follows: 'It is distinguished by its utter simplicity, lack of excrescences, smooth and solid surfaces; its tendency towards smooth unbroken lines and surfaces; solidity, practicability and comfort; also by its new and unusual woods, inlays of ivory and metal, untraditional designs in upholstery fabrics and all sorts of new materials never before employed in decoration.'

Almost all innovations in furniture at this time were the work of architects, from Mies van der Rohe and Breuer to LeCorbusier and Alvar Aalto, because no suitable furniture existed for their architecture. Such was not the case with German emigré Walter von Nessen. Before leaving Germany in 1919, von Nessen had studied with Bruno Paul. He set up the Nessen studio in New York in 1927 as a small family business with an emphasis on lamps.

Combining the elements of Bauhaus design with French and Austrian neoclassicism inspired by the Paris Exposition, he created a more economical and practical furniture. Instead of using precious substances like silver and crystal or expensive woods, von Nessen took advantage of the compounds modern technology was making available. These included the popular new plastic Bakelite and, especially, chromium, which was seen as the modern sub-

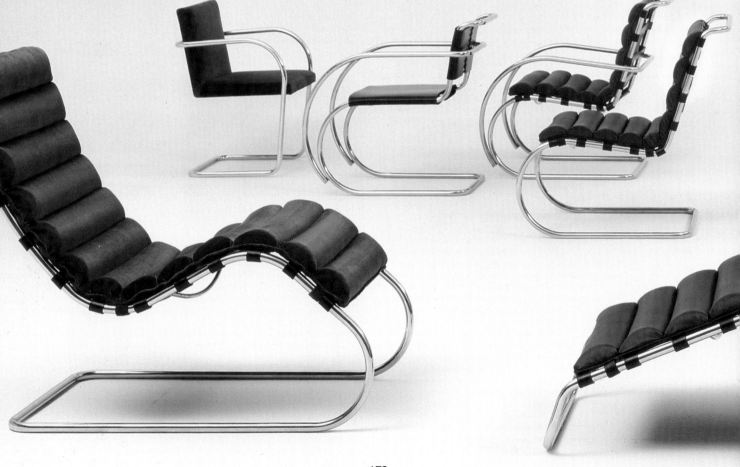

Above: *The Barcelona collection of Mies van der Rohe.*   Below: *Cantilever furniture by Mies van der Rohe.*

stitute for silver: less expensive and polish-free. Although German by birth, his American approach to furniture design is evident in the emphasis on practicality and marketability.

Another furniture designer who united Bauhaus concepts with the influence of the Paris Exposition was Gilbert Rohde. Although he did not participate in the Metropolitan Exhibition in 1929, his work was marketed by Lord & Taylor, and the New York penthouse he designed for Norman Lee got exposure both nationally and abroad. Rohde's drum table, called the 'rotorette,' had rotating shelves which could be used for books or liquor.

In 1930 Rohde made a trip to Grand Rapids, Michigan, then the country's furniture capital, to sell his designs. Although the Depression hampered his success, he established an important association with a furniture company, Herman Miller. The company's president, D J DePree, hired Rohde in 1931 to develop new designs for space-saving and multipurpose furniture. It was a daring step in those dark days and signaled the pioneering role the company would play in the development of modern American furniture.

Rohde was one of the first to put on the market the Bakelite top tables with chrome-plated legs which typify furniture of the era for so many. The success of Rohde's furniture in Chicago led the Herman Miller Company to concentrate exclusively on modern furniture. In

Dining Room by Donald Deskey, 1934 Special Exhibition.

contrast, prevailing dogma may have been reflected in the exclusion of architect Frank Lloyd Wright from the exposition.

The exaggerated ornateness of Art Deco style furniture began to soften in the 1930s. *The International Style* by Henry Russell Hitchcock and Philip Johnson, the 1932 catalog for an exhibit at the new Museum of Modern Art in New York, established new criteria for architecture and

would have an impact on furniture design. These criteria consisted of a concern for the enclosure of space, of regularity rather than symmetry and, in divergence with Art Deco, a rejection of arbitrary surface decoration.

By 1933, the Nazis had shut down the Bauhaus. Soon members of the Bauhaus began to arrive in America. Marcel Breuer, working with the unit furniture which had standardized dimensions so it could be combined according to varying needs and space, appeared alongside Donald Deskey and Gilbert Rohde in the 'Design for Living' house at the 1933 Century of Progress Exposition in Chicago.

If the Depression kept the American public from buying the new furniture, that didn't mean they couldn't look. There were many expositions and fairs which allowed them to do that. Fed by the bleakness of the times, designers' visions of a future in which art and technololgy, furniture and the machine, were united provided spiritual nourishment and the theme for exhibits. Rohde's 'Furniture for a Man's Den' appeared at the 1932 'Design for the Machine' exhibit at the Philadelphia Museum. At the second Metropolitan Museum of Art design exhibition in 1934, he displayed an innovative if not very popular chrome-legged piano.

Department stores continued to showcase the latest in furniture with 7000 people a day passing through Macy's 'Magic Rooms.' There were

A Paldao wood-and-myrtle-burl desk bookcase designed by Gilbert Rohde for Herman Miller, circa 1935.

also exhibits at Lord & Taylor and Halle's in Cleveland. Gilbert Rohde designed a series of furniture groups for Wanamaker's in New York and Philadelphia called 'Modern Village.' While they were successful at generating sales, the clerks' lack of understanding of the new furniture led Rohde to develop the concept of independent showrooms which catered directly to architects and designers.

The museum of Modern Art in New York

Left to right: *A Dining Room by Eugene Schoen, a Dining Room by Walter Downs Teague, A Music Room corner by Gilbert Rohde, and a Room for a Lady by Eliel Saarinen, all designed for Special Exhibitions.*

A Saarinen armchair, recalling the early tub chairs, has an inlaid exterior.

entered the arena decisively in 1934 with an influential exhibition, 'Machine Art.' The name was quickly adopted as the general term for furniture of the era. Organized by Philip Johnson, the MOMA exhibition had lofty aims. The catalog proclaimed: 'In Plato's day the tools were simple handworker's implements, but today, as a result of the perfection of modern materials and the precision of modern instruments the modern machine-made object approaches far more closely and more frequently those pure shapes the contemplation of which Plato calls the first of the "pure pleasures".'

If such sentiments seemed heady stuff, the new museum was determined to influence taste. Machine art furniture began to evolve toward a freer use of compound curves and sculpted shapes in contrast to the earlier emphasis on geometry. Primary was the adaptation of industrial materials. Furniture was slipjointed, bolted or welded to form continuous, seamless contours and reduce design to its simplest form.

The International style in architecture helped move furniture away from the exotic, expres-

sionist qualities of Art Deco toward severer forms almost devoid of ornament and color. The machine, however, continued to be mythologized and romanticized. Important to the average American household as any piece of furniture in the 1930s was the radio, and television, the modern miracle, was waiting in the wings.

By the time television was introduced at the New York World's Fair in 1939, modern furniture had lost the square, linear look of early Art Deco. Furniture in the Highway and Horizons building by architect Norman Bel Geddes was notable for its rounded corners and sleek edges. Streamlining was also evident in the work of Walter Teague, Raymond Loewy and Henry Dreyfuss. The country's new mobility was having its impact, and Bel Geddes, along with Richard Buckminster Fuller, whose geodesic dome design made him famous much later, was a proponent of airflow design.

Wind-tunnel research had shown that the

The coconut chair produced by Herman Miller had a seat, arms and back molded in one piece.

A tubular steel bed with a silver lacquer finish designed by Ruth Reeves in the late 1920s.

teardrop shape, which cut down wind resistance on moving objects, was the proper design for vehicles. The teardrop shape also suggested motion in stationary objects and was adopted in furniture. Raymond Loewy's designs for airplanes and trains typified the streamlining look and the 'Dynamic Office Desk' produced by Art Metal in 1936 had rounded corners and smooth sides. In addition to teardrop shapes, Streamline furniture featured flaring and decorative parallel lines called speed whiskers. Russel Wright – better known for his Art Deco dishware – was one of those who popularized streamlined furniture, producing an 'American Modern' group of bleached maple in 1935.

An important design element developing concurrently in modern furniture was Scandinavian. After the 1930 Stockholm exhibition, the Scandinavians had continued to produce furniture with an emphasis on natural wood, purity of form and balance in proportion which would influence American furniture. In contrast to the Bauhaus tradition, the Scandinavian credo called for no change in form unless demanded by function.

Danish architect and designer Kaare Klint, who founded the Department of Furniture at the Danish Academy of Art, had developed studies of proportion based on the interrelationship of people and furniture as early as 1917. By the mid-1920s, Danish architects and cabinetmakers joined forces to establish a series of furniture competitions which insured a tradition of high quality functionalist modern furniture.

The Finnish architect and designer Alvar

Aalto had been experimenting with molded plywood, capitalizing on the natural springiness of the medium. He was given credit in architecture for humanizing the austere international style of the 1930s through an emphasis on organic forms and the use of wood. Among other objects, he produced a chair of bent plywood on a tubular metal frame in 1932 and marketed it through Artek, the firm he founded to mass produce furniture for the United States and Britain as well as Scandinavia.

As World War II edged closer, some of the most influential European furniture designers emigrated to the United States. Bauhaus

A lounge chair upholstered in zebra, by Alvar Aalto, has supporting arms made of molded plywood.

Above: *The womb chairs of Eero Saarinen have upholstered shells on steel rod frames.*

Below: *Scandinavian influence is seen in the use of light and highly polished wood.*

founder Walter Gropius went to the School of Architecture at Harvard in 1937, along with Marcel Breuer. Ludwig Mies van der Rohe joined the Illinois Institute of Technology, which constructivist Moholy-Nagy had founded as the New Bauhaus.

In 1939 under the continuing tutelage of Gilbert Rohde, the Herman Miller Company opened a showroom in the Chicago Merchandise Mart with a system of desk tops, pedestals and drawers that could be combined in 452 different ways. In addition to unit furniture, Rohde had introduced the company to metal furniture, as well as sectional furniture and office furniture. This designer was at perhaps the peak of his career for the 1939 World's Fair in New York. He served on the committee which planned the fair's layout, and his work appeared in the Focal Exhibition on Community Affairs, the Anthracite Industries exhibition, a bedroom for the 'Unit of Living' apartment and the Rohm & Haas display for Plexiglas and Crystolite.

Another organization that had gained momentum by the late 1930s was the Cranbrook

Above: *William Haines trimmed a leather-covered chair with a leather band in 1939.*

Academy in Bloomfield Hills, Michigan. Established in the mid-1920s by newspaper publisher and philanthropist George G Booth and directed by Eliel Saarinen, its goal was to create an artistic community which integrated fine arts with the crafts.

Many of those who came to Cranbrook, including Harry Bertoia, Ray Kaiser, Charles Eames, Florence Schust and Benjamin Baldwin, went on to produce important works of modern furniture. Through her marriage to Hans Knoll, Florence Schust entered a partnership in the Knoll furniture company, started in 1939, which was to have an even more major influence on American furniture than Herman Miller.

The 1941 competition at the Museum of Modern Art called 'Organic Design in Home Furnishing' signaled the beginning of a new preeminence for modern American furniture. It was organized by MOMA's first director of Industrial Design, Alfred Noyes. Although the title for the exhibit was perhaps confusing, the emphasis on Bauhaus-derived functionalism was clear. 'Organic,' by Noyes definition, was

'an harmonious organization of the parts within the whole, according to structure, material and purpose.' Reflecting a typically American cooperation between the art and commercial worlds, the idea for the exhibit had originated with Bloomingdale's store in New York.

Cranbrook colleagues Charles Eames, who had arrived at the school as a student in 1938, and Eero Saarinen, architect son of the director, collaborated on a new form of plywood shell to create sectional and lounge chairs, which won top prizes in the MOMA 1940-1941 competition. The shells were molded in two directions, rather than bent in one direction as furniture by Marcel Breuer and Alvar Aalto had been. This resulted in chairs which appeared sculptured.

The furniture for which Charles Eames is most famous was a chair developed in 1946. Its molded plywood back has been described as a rectangle about to turn into an oval. Several versions of the Eames chair were exhibited at the Museum of Modern Art's 1946 show, 'One Hundred Useful Objects of Fine Design.' Its distinctively American feel comes from the simplicity of design combined with a frankness

The Bruno chair is also designed on the cantilever principle.

Above: *Sculptor Isamu Noguchi designed a coffee table of glass with an abstract base.*
Below: *A side chair with the legs repeating the angle of the seat and back designed by Pierre Jeanneret, circa 1949.*

of mechanical detail. The Eames chair epitomizes the contributions of American design to furniture history. Underlying its design is the philosophy that there is an inherent good in making the fullest use of the least material. Two other key components to the American philosophy as represented by the Eames chair are democracy and industrialization. The American ideal is for a furniture available for everyone which capitalizes on the latest techniques in technology and mass production. Gone was the heavily upholstered look prevalent since the nineteenth century. Functionalist furniture like the Eames chair had an affinity for the free-flowing shapes and abstract designs of modern sculpture. It curved to fit the body and incorporated space, the parts on occasion seeming to hover in the air like a Calder mobile. The molded forms recalled the way an auto body is stamped in a die press.

The Eames chair showed the extent of the changes that life in America had undergone. Modern transportation meant not only that Americans traveled more, but also packed up and moved more often. Moving demanded furniture that was smaller, more portable and adaptable. Storage components began to be

Above: *A sofa designed by Eames has foam padding over the contoured frame.*

Below: *The 'Eames Chair' uses molded and contoured plywood on a metal frame.*

Above: *Harry Bertoia designed a chair whose diamond shape is echoed in the individual units that make up the whole.*
Below: *Bertoia's rectangular chair could be upholstered over the wire frame.*

absorbed by architecture. Houses were becoming smaller, and the relationship between indoors and outdoors was changing. Electronics began to alter ideas about objects. The geometric shapes of Machine Art in the 1930s had suggested the mechanical action of push-pull; electronics required an understanding of invisible forces.

Gilbert Rohde was succeeded at Herman Miller by George Nelson. The storage system Nelson produced in 1948 had interchangeable sections, as did the cabinets designed by Charles Eames for Herman Miller in 1950. Architectural in appearance and function but not built in, they were important as the first cabinets to forsake traditional construction entirely for the techniques used in industrial products. Another difficult furniture problem, the well-designed individual light, was solved by Isamu Noguchi's cylindrical Akari lamp, make in 1948 for Knoll.

The Museum of Modern Art held a 'Competition for Low-Cost Furniture Design' in 1948. Charles Eames contributed an asymmetrical lounge chair and a molded armchair. Eames' Cranbrook colleague Eero Saarinen produced his womb chair, an extension of the ideas begun in the chairs which won the 1941 'Organic Design' competition.

Scandinavian concepts continued to have an impact on American furniture design in the post-war 1940s. The occupation of Denmark in 1940 had meant the closing of that country's borders, but the collaboration between Danish architects and cabinetmakers continued. A reaction set in against early functionalist severity and the Klint school, and by the late 1940s, Danish furniture design flowered in a new Art Nouveau-like interest in sculptured effects. Since exporting was important, Scandinavians were among the first to mass produce furniture which could be knocked down for transport. In Sweden in the late 1940s, research resulted in standardized construction techniques and an interest in functional anatomy.

The association of furniture designers fostered by Cranbrook Academy was extended by Florence Knoll through the Knoll Furniture company. At the Detroit Institute of Arts exhibit 'For Modern Living' in 1949, Knoll herself exhibited furniture which domesticated designs from the Barcelona pavilion. These included washable plastic, leather and jute furniture and scratch- and burn-resistant butcher block tables.

Jens Risom's chair uses fabric webbing over a wooden frame.

The Saarinen pedestal table was first introduced in 1955.

It was not simply the Cranbrook connection which gave the Knoll Company its leadership position in modern American furniture. Probably because of her own talent, Florence Knoll had a knack for attracting designers of international reputation. She found a middle ground between the traditional designers and the modernists. Knoll began producing van der Rohe's Barcelona chair in 1948. Other Knoll-produced designs include Marcel Breuer's chairs, Isamu Noguchi's Akari lamp and Harry Bertoia's wire Diamond chair. The company also manufactured Eero Saarinen's pedestal furniture and George Nakashima's Conoid chair.

Harry Bertoia, who served as a metal craftsman for Cranbrook, worked primarily as a sculptor. He created furniture for a while, however, and his lounge chair and ottoman were made by Knoll and exhibited at the Museum of Modern Art in 1952-1953. He suggested that, like cellular structures, the design evolved naturally from organic principles.

Eames continued to turn out dramatically new designs in the 1950s, the best known of which are his lounge chair and ottoman of 1956, made of molded plywood with leather. That the history of modern American furniture sounds like the story of chair design reflects modern American lifestyles, as well as the fact that the chair presents designers with their greatest challenges.

While the Eames chair of 1946 provided the benchmark for the 1940s, it was Eero Saarinen's

Above: *An Eames lounge chair and ottoman have pedestal bases*

Below: *Pedestal tables and chairs prove the success of Saarinen's attempt to clear up the 'slums of legs.'*

Contemporary designs are equally at home as office furniture.

white pedestal chairs and tables that were the hallmark of the 1950s. Saarinen began working on the concept of single-unit molded plastic furniture whoch would be clear of the 'slum of legs' in 1953. Pedestal bases provided the solution, although it was necessary to cast them in aluminium since plastic was not yet strong enough. The idea was complete by 1955, and Knoll began producing pedestal furniture soon after. The technique of molding or stamping had begun to push furniture in the direction of unified, one-piece design, and Saarinen's design was the closest yet to that ideal.

The Museum of Modern Art, under the leadership of Edgar Kauffmann Jr in the first half of the 1950s, continued to exert a powerful influence on furniture design. The years from 1950 to 1955 saw a series of 'Good Design' exhibitions which sought to influence wholesale buyers and manufacturers as well as encourage good design work. The exhibits brought recognition to many new designers, like Edward Wormley, who had worked for Dunbar Furniture since the 1930s. Greta von Nessen, who succeeded her husband after his death, showed her 'Anywhere' lamp at the 1952 'Good Design' exhibit.

One of the most successful designers of the 1950s was Paul McCobb, who appeared regularly in the 'Good Design' exhibits. In 1957, Bloomingdale's featured a Paul McCobb Shop with 15 different rooms. His work typified the new American style: clean, low lines; natural wood, foam cushions; modular furniture; room dividers, and wall systems known as 'living walls.'

If the Museum of Modern Art seemed too elitist for the woman in the street, *House and Garden's Complete Guide to Home Decoration* informed her that 'modern' was out. The proper term now was 'contemporary.' Functionalism had been extended from the object itself to its manufacture, distribution and maintenance. Mass production, making possible the manufacture of enormous quantities of furniture which meant an enormous number of customers must want the same object, had profoundly altered attitudes.

The notion that visible form must transparently display the logic of its function was growing obsolete. Lightweight nylons and plastics were changing the relationship between weight and size, leading to new and unconventional shapes. Permanence was being replaced by relativism, and the Museum of Modern Art found itself at odds with an industry which promoted novelty for the sake of marketing, when MOMA argued against alteration without functional justification.

At the Aspen International Design Conference in 1957, designer Richard Latham created a stir by questioning the standards of MOMA's 'Good Design' shows. Rayner Banham suggested it was absurd to demand that objects designed for a short life exhibit qualities of eternal validity. The throw-away culture was about to be born, and a number of other currents were gathering strength. Ergonomics, the science of biotechnology, had been developed during World War II, and was making its mark. Raymond Loewy's DO/MORE posture chair was introduced in 1956, and Henry Dreyfuss published a book on human engineering called *Designing for People*. The groundwork was also being laid for a shift in the seat of power to Italy, via the Milan Triennale exhibitions of the 1950s.

The shape of Harry Bertoia's furniture is accentuated by the pattern of the rug and the angularity of the sculpture.

An arm chair by Charles Pollock combines the pedestal base, the molded seat and the tubular steel arms.

The turning point would be the 1964 Triennale, with its leisure time theme, touting lightness, transparency and color. The marriage of aesthetics and technology conceived in the nineteenth century was beginning to disintegrate.

Countercurrents, which had existed all along but not been given their due, won increasing recognition. Brancusi-trained sculptor Isamu Noguchi, for example, had been creating organic furniture since the 1940s, including a free-form coffee table with glass top for Herman Miller in 1944 and a rocking stool-table in 1954 for Knoll. Wharton Esherick had been making unconventional, free-form one-of-a-kind furniture since the 1940s. His spiral oak stairway of 1930 could have been right at home alongside the new work that began to appear. Another designer, George Nakashima, produced furniture that incorporated natural forms. His Conoid chair, produced in 1962, reflected a rejection of the machine age and the space age.

Marc Harrison, the Cranbrook designer of the Cuisinart, specialized in ergonomics, and another Cranbrook graduate, David Rowland, explored the use of steel and plastic finishes. His 40-in-4 stacking chairs won the Grand Prize at the 1964 Milan Triennale. Richard Schultz, who

had worked with Harry Bertoia, and had been a member of the Knoll Design Development Group, produced a chaise longue of aluminum, vinyl and Dacron webbing in 1966 for Knoll. It won the 1967 AID (International Design Award). Warren Platner designed an upholstered chair and ottoman with a steel wire base for Knoll in 1966 which won the AID award that year.

During the tumultuous 1960s, the Museum of Modern Art no longer was able to set the standard for American furniture. A new interest in the handcrafting of one-of-a-kind furniture emerged in the 1960s, spawning what has been called the Early Craft Revival. The individual's involvement in the making and buying of furniture began to be seen as a remedy for the spiritual impoverishment caused by a mechanized and depersonalized society. By the mid-1960s, Wendell Castle developed a sculptural style called Biomorphic that seemed to be in the vanguard. It rejected traditional notions of furniture as constructed of boards in favor of furniture carved from solid wood or laminated in shapes suggesting nature. Reflecting the mood of the times, Biomorphic furniture followed an anti-rational, anti-industrial aesthetic

The back and seat are one piece of molded wood, and the arms are made from another, in this armchair attributed to George Mulhauser.

Cast-plastic chairs became popular in the 1970s. These, designed by Verner Panton, can easily be stacked for storage.

in opposition to American designers continuing to work with the industry, to the Italians in Milan and, ultimately, to High Tech.

Meanwhile, Bill Stephens, working for Knoll International, created handsome new hybrids of old and new methods and materials in the late 1960s. George Nelson designed a classic sling sofa of chrome and leather in 1964 for Herman Miller. The Danish designer Verner Panton solved the problem of single-piece design with his award-winning stacking chair of polyester and fiberglass which Herman Miller manufactured. The title of the 1964 International Design Conference at Aspen seemed to reflect the uncertainty of the times. It was called 'Design '64: Directions and Dilemmas.'

The effect of Pop Art on furniture in the mid-1960s was anarchic but consistent with the mood of the decade. The movement's credo was based on a refusal to ignore the transitory or to reject the marginal. Pop artist Claes Oldenburg, who had been creating 'art' objects out of toasters, typewriters and telephones, exhibited a bedroom set at the Sidney Janis Gallery in New York in the winter of 1963. It consisted of a 'modern' bed, dresser and chair with accessories and helped bury for good the ossified functionalist notion of what was modern. Not long after, new furniture styles began to be described as post-modern. Despite the impact on the art world of the Pop artists, the impact of Pop on furniture seemed to come primarily

through Italy. The Milan group DePas, D'Urbino, Lomazzi developed an inflatable 'Blow' chair in 1967 and a giant catcher's mitt called the 'Joe' chair in 1970. Gatti, Paolini, Teodoro, also of Italy, in 1969 produced the 'Sacco' chair, which was the prototype for bean-bag furniture which gained popularity for a time in the United States. An American version of the disposable ethic exemplified by Pop Art was Frank Gehry's 1972 'Easy Edges' rocking chair, made of cardboard.

Called the 'Me' decade by historians, the 1970s seemed to lack a single cohesive furniture style, unless the variety of approaches were collectively labeled the 'Personal.' Tage Frid, who settled in Rhode Island after leaving Denmark in 1948 and setting up the woodworking program for the School for American Craftsmen, had already produced a three-legged stool with a seat only six inches wide in 1965. In 1979 he introduced a chair using the klismos form of classical Greek furniture. The furniture of Sam Maloof represented some of the best of the decade. His 1974 rocking chair with ribbed slats originally was designed for a woman with a bad back. The drop-leaf table with chair that Maloof designed in 1971 demonstrated a characteristic affinity with nature through its emphasis on the wood grain. James Krenov, working at the College of the Redwoods, characterized the 1970s California Roundover style, which was in some ways like a chunky version of Scandinavian Modern.

Biomorphic furniture continued to appear in David Crawford's Flying Lizard Rocker and John Economaki's Executive Desk. By the late 1970s, however, its formulator, Wendell Castle, abandoned the Biomorphic style. His Double Chair-back Settee retained the rounded sculptured forms of the earlier style but combined them with a new crispness. Castle's Card Table with Hat and Briefcase spoofed American Chippendale, recalling the statements of Pop Art at the same time that it commented on the renewed interest of 1970s furniture designers in early periods. Judy Kensley McKie seemed to combine practicality with fantasy in an almost formal mode with her interesting 1979 'Bench with Horses'.

The decade of the 1980s opened with an energy crisis which made plastic furniture less economically appealing. Conservation, ecology, product safety, durability and human engineering were all high on the agenda for a generation of furniture designers who at the 1970 International Design Conference in Aspen had demanded a 11-point resolution covering issues from Vietnam and abortion to rejection of the profit motive in furniture-making. The success of Italian furniture design, built on an ability to adapt new materials and processes, continued late in the 1970s with the emergence of the 'Memphis' group.

As America moved through the last quarter of the twentieth century, furniture design seemed more varied, more creative, more American than ever. American furniture design had come a long way from the days of the late 1920s and before, when it was still looking over its shoulder toward Europe. The wealth of ideas which came with the waves of immigration had been assimilated. A new, distinctly American style of furniture had emerged in the 1940s and 1950s. Built on the supremacy of American technology and industry, it instilled in American design a confidence which carried it through the social upheavals of the 1960s and could accommodate the many directions of the 1970s and 1980s. Throughout, modern American furniture sustained a tradition of egalitarianism, simplicity and practicality at the same time that it left room for the individual, for the spirit and for beauty. And to the extent that it succeeded, contemporary Americans were carrying on the tradition that had begun some 350 years ago, a tradition that could be said to give a coherent theme and pattern to the history of American furniture.

A modern side chair by Danish-born designer Tage Frid was inspired by the ancient Greek klismos.

A modern walnut rocker by Sam Maloof has ribbed slats and extended rockers.

Index

Acknowledgments

The author and publisher would like to thank the following people who have helped in the preparation of this book: Janet Bond, Wendy Murphy, Broos Rhodes and Joel Zoss, who contributed to the history; Elizabeth Montgomery who edited it; Richard Garratt who designed it; John Bowman and Mary Raho who did the picture research; Cynthia Klein who prepared the index.

Picture credits

The Adirondack Museum, Blue Mountain Lake, NY: 138B. American Philosophical Society: 55B. Arkitectura: 171TL, 176T. The Art Museum, Princeton University – Gift of Roland Rohlfs: 155R. The Art Institute of Chicago: 154L – Mrs Theodore Tieken Gift; 155mid – Gift of Mrs Philip K Wrigley; 158L – The Graham Foundation; 158R – Gift of Mr and Mrs F M Farenwald; 159R – Antiquarian Society through Mrs William P Bogess II Gift. Aurora Colony Historical Society: 120B. Boscobel Restoration, Inc: 62, 72-3. Brooklyn Museum: 92-3 and 98-9 – Gift of Sarah Milligan Rand, Kate Milligan Brill and the Dick S Ramsey Fund; 104L, 109, 111 – Gift of Eleanor Curnow; 105, 108L – Gift of Mrs Ernest Vietor; 114L, Gift of Susan D Bliss; 130-1, 132 – Gift of John D Rockefeller Jr and John D Rockefeller III; 137L – Gift of Herbert Hemphill; 139B – The Woodward Memorial Fund; 143 – Gift of the Estate of Mrs William H Good; 146L – H Randolph Lever Fund. Chicago Architecture Foundation: 161B, 162. Both pictures © H K Barnett. Chicago Historical Society: 134, 168 both, 169T. Christie's: 2-3, 11, 12, 18R, 38, 39, 4z4, 49, 50T, 57T, 69, 70 both, 151, 157TR, 159L, 161T, 175T, 177T. Chrysler Museum, Norfolk VA – Gift of Walter P Chrysler: 154-5. The Cooper-Hewitt Museum, The Smithsonian Institution: 160T, 171B. Cooper-Union, NY, NY: 127. Essex Institute, Salem MA: 19R, 22, 60, 115R. Gamble House,

Pasadena CA: 163, 164. Collection of Mr and Mrs Henry D Green: 63, 76. The Henry Ford Museum and Greenfield Village: 88T, 101, 116B, 135 both. Hancock Shaker Village, Inc., Pittsfield MA: 1, 117 both, 120TL and R, 121 both. Hitchcock Chair Co.: 114-5, 115B. Independence National Historical Park Collection: 54L and R. International Contract Furnishings, Inc.: 117B. Johnson Wax: 160BR. Jordan-Volpe Gallery, NY, NY: 145L, 146R, 147 all, 148 both, 149, 153, 156L, 157L, 160BR. Knoll International: 4-5, 170B, 172-3, 178 both, 179B, 180B, 182 both, 183 both, 184B, 185, 186, 187L. The Metropolitan Museum of Art, NY, NY: 13, 16B, 18L, 21, 26-7, 30, 42, 43, 80TL, 81, 82B, 85T, 102, 106-7, 144, 156R, 170TL and R, 171TR, 174 all, 175BR. Herman Miller, Inc.: 176B, 180T, 181 both, 184T, 188. Missouri Historical Society: 85B. Mount Vernon Ladies Assn: 58-9, 61R. Munson-Proctor-Williams Institute, Utica, NY, Proctor Collection: 103. Museum of the City of New York: 132, 133. Museum of Early Southern Decorative Arts: 23, 53T, 90. Museum of Fine Arts, Boston, MA: 19L, 36, 56, 79, 145R, 189L and R. Museum of New Mexico: 119T, 122B. National Trust for Historic Preservation: 96. The Newark Museum: 108R, 110, 112, 113T. New York State Office of Parks, recreation and Historic Preservation, Olana: 129. Plimoth Plantation, Plymouth, MA: 6-7. Rockefeller Center, 166-7, 169B. Rutherford B Hayes Presidential Center: 123T, 125T. San Antonio Museum Assn, San Antonio, TX: 140T. Shelburne Museum, Shelburne, VT: 40. © 1985 Sotheby-Parke-Bernet, Inc.: 10, 14, 16T, 17, 20, 47T, 52, 66 both, 74, 78, 82T, 86, 95, 126, 139T. Smithsonian Institution: 94, 107, 137R, 138T, 140R, 141, 142. Margaret Woodbury Strong Museum: 128 both, 136R. State Museum of Pennsylvania, Pennsylvania Historical and Museum Commission: 68, 87. Vesterheim, Norwegian-American Museum, Decorah, IA: 124, 125B. Virginia Museum of Fine Arts: 24, 34, 37, 45 both, 47B, 50L, 51L, 53, 57B, 61L, 64, 65, 71, 75, 77, 83, 91, 97, 100, 104R, 113B, 116T, 152, 154mid. Wadsworth Atheneum, Hartford, CT: 9, 15, 123B. The Henry Francis duPont Winterthur Museum: 28-9, 32-3, 46, 84-5, 88B, 89. Yale University Art Gallery: 72, 80BR – The Mabel Brady Garvan Collection; 136L – Gift of Mr and Mrs Samuel Schwartz; 150 – Bequest of Shepherd Stevens.